The
GATEKEEPER

The Television Series
Robert J. Thompson, *Series Editor*

THE
GATEKEEPER

My Thirty Years as a TV Censor

ALFRED R. SCHNEIDER

with **Kaye Pullen**

With a Foreword by Michael Dann

Syracuse University Press

First Edition 2001

02 03 04 05 06 07   6 5 4 3 2

The paper used in this publication meets the minimum requirements
of American National Standard for Information Sciences—Permanence of Paper
for Printed Library Materials, ANSI Z39.48-1984.∞™

Library of Congress Cataloging-in-Publication Data

Schneider, Alfred R.
The gatekeeper : my 30 years as a TV censor / Alfred R. Schneider, with Kaye Pullen.
p. cm. — (The television series)
ISBN 0-8156-0683-4 (alk. paper)
1. Schneider, Alfred R. 2. Television broadcasting—United States—Biography.
3. Executives—United States—Biography. 4. Television—Censorship—United States.
I. Pullen, Kaye. II. Title. III. Series.
PN1992.4.S28 A3 2001
384.55'092—dc21   00-061249

Manufactured in the United States of America

For Jane
and for Lee, Jeff, and Liz

Alfred R. Schneider is an attorney/consultant in the communications industry with thirty-five years of experience in the broadcasting business. He has supervised the Broadcast Standards and Practices department, was vice president in charge of administration for the ABC Television Network, and was senior member of the National Association of Broadcasters' Code Review Board, on which he served for twenty years. Schneider held the position of vice president, Policy and Standards, Capital Cities/ABC, from February 1986 until his retirement in April 1991. A Phi Beta Kappa graduate of Hamilton College (1949), he is a graduate of Harvard Law School (1952) and is a member of the New York State Bar.

Kaye Pullen, a freelance writer and communications consultant, lives in Philadelphia where she is active in the arts community as a teacher and poet. A native of Tennessee, Pullen was a speechwriter for President Gerald R. Ford, an executive at ABC Telvision, and a newspaper editorial writer and columnist. She was graduated magna cum laude from the University of Memphis (1966) and received her M.A. from the University of Minnesota.

Contents

Foreword
MICHAEL DANN   ix

Preface   xiii

Overview   1

Violence   11

Sex   27

Editing Theatrical Movies for Television   46

Movies Made for Television   56

Programs Designed for Children   74

Special Interest Advocacy   89

The "Family Viewing Hour"   100

A Television Ratings System   115

Speaking the Truth
   Preserving the Integrity of the Docudrama   122

Censorship and the Censor's Role   131

Notes   145

Index   149

Foreword

MICHAEL DANN

For the past fifty-two years I have been involved in programming for television. I headed the program departments at NBC and CBS. I have been a consultant in the programming area for other networks including ABC and the BBC and have originated programs for telecast. During this half century, I have worked closely with producers and writers in getting programs on the air. During my entire career, I don't think I ever was involved with a program where the censor, for one reason or another, was not involved in the content of the show and its production prior to air.

The importance of this book—the first book written, to my knowledge, from the inside perspective of the censor—is to show the problems and difficulties in presenting controversial subjects, scenes, and language on television. The censor had enough power to make my job very difficult. If I were the head of all programming or the executive in charge of daytime soaps or late night entertainment, it was incumbent upon me to maintain a relationship with the censor that would permit me to exercise the widest latitude possible. It was often a fragile relationship.

The censor was a man who had to say "no" an awful lot. That was his professional job. Sometimes he would have to say no against his own personal desires and act solely as the umpire. The objective in the program department was to get the umpire on its side. And it could only get him/her on its side if he was persuaded early enough *before* an issue became truly important. If the controversy got into the newspapers or sponsors became involved, the problem would always escalate. We had a rule at the networks: "the sooner you got the censor into the act, the better your chances of getting it on the air."

Alfred Schneider was widely accepted as the most respected censor in the industry. He held the post for many years at ABC. As a network latecomer ABC did an awful lot of creative and innovative programming that the other networks did not have to do. They took more risks and put much more responsibility in the hands of producers: that fact made Schneider's job all the more difficult. At the time, ABC was considered the producers' network. There was a Code Review Board then under the auspices of the Nation Association of Broadcasters (NAB). Schneider became its senior member in the early 1970's, and then its longest running member. The Code set standards that were observed by all the networks and stations that were members. Often Schneider's leadership affected what was done at the other networks.

I have known the author for many years. He held the post of chief censor for longer than anybody and was involved in more program sessions than any other nonprogram executive. His decisions have affected program acceptability as well as questions of language and picture.

I have participated, argued, and contributed to the changing television morality in both content and taste over these many years. Schneider describes many similar experiences. I can remember *The Kraft Theater* telecast in 1951 when the word *pregnant* was not acceptable in a script. The Program Practice people, the censor, said to us, "You cannot use the word 'pregnant,' but you can add a line to the script that says you are adding another room to the house or are converting the office to a bedroom for a newcomer and that would connote that the family was about to have a baby." So you always involved the censor in your planning to make life easier and to do your job effectively.

The 1950s were a picnic compared to the rapid changes that took place in the 1960s and 1970s. It was no longer a matter of fighting about words and phrases but content. Television went through two different changes in content. One had to do with the blue collar kind of show where for the first time we introduced characters such as Archie in *All in the Family*, Maude in *Maude*, and *The Jeffersons* and *Sanford and Son*. Then the programming debates dealt with the situations these personalities found themselves in, which were much more realistic than say those which involved characters in *The Beverly Hillbillies* or *Petticoat Junction* or *Green Acres*. Certain shows, such as *The Smothers Brothers* on CBS and *Soap* on ABC, were designed at the very beginning to deal with the real world in terms of social and political satire. By design they shocked the audience with their relevance and language. The question between the program people and the censor came down to what could we get away with. Every single script and every single episode became a crisis.

The producer wanted a controversial show that would attract large audiences. The program department always supported the producer. Tommy Smothers, for example, would create dialogue or situations that he knew the censors would object to—often to upset them or to use as a negotiating tool. Sometimes he would say to me, "Oh, I thought you'd take that out.

We didn't want to use it. It's a prank." On the other hand, we took him seriously and fought the censor. Our job was to support the producer or the performer. They deliver the ratings. They deliver the audience. They deliver the laughs or tears. Our ability to live with the producer is our primary responsibility; the censor's task is to monitor the rules he or she has created.

While Alfred Schneider was guided by the rules of the moment, I knew he was also influenced by the constant and dramatic changes taking place during this period. While we did move along, we in television were not the ones to initiate change as to what was acceptable or permissible. Television, unlike movies, and books, and Broadway, was never in the vanguard of any crusade to use four-letter words or to depict nonmarried households or to show specific scenes of sexual activity. Movies, books, and the theater did "it" first.

Schneider's book gives an in-depth look at how we did advance the agenda and the dramatic changes as they took place. He also describes his on-the-scene experiences of the conflict between programmer and censor, which always remained volatile, even as the rules changed. For example, I remember when the late Herbert Brodkin did a show called *The Nurses* and he wanted to show the actual birth of a baby. He was told it could not be done. Brodkin said he would not do the program series unless he could show the actual birth. Programming finally prevailed and a birth was shown. It may have been somewhat differently than has since been permitted many times on television, but for all practical purposes a baby was shown being delivered from the mother.

Schneider's battle and perspective differed from mine as a programmer, but I vividly recall the grief and upset caused by controversial programs dealing with relevant issues of the 1960s and 1970s. Television started to deal with dramas like *The Defenders* that highlighted a political or social issue of the week. When Reginald Rose was story editor, he looked for scripts that dealt with subjects of exceptional importance. As the hour drama replaced the half-hour drama and movies for television gained popularity, some very serious problems of that day such as drug addiction, single parenthood, alcohol abuse, the Vietnam War, homosexuality, and interpersonal relationships came to the fore. One famous show called *The People Next Door* dealt with a young couple living in Greenwich Village who were attracted to each other because of their need for drugs. The story was developed as a searing indictment of drug use and the destructive effect such use had on teenagers. The censor, for the first time, accepted a scene such as the one showing the young unmarried couple making love together in bed, because the show demonstrated the evils of drug use. And, of course, at CBS there was the enormous controversy generated by the abortion show on *Maude*.

So many of the controversies I remember and those described by Schneider reflect the many changes in programming. This book marks a distinctive era in the growth of television. The censor today in the twenty-first century has far less authority than Schneider did in those thirty years that he chronicles. So much programming is spontaneous, live, and unrehearsed. Talk shows carried in the daytime and late at night, for example, are very difficult to control and edit. Also there is no real program censorship on cable. Cable is far more liberal. We have whole channels that are dedicated solely to content totally unacceptable to the television networks. While the six major networks still maintain departments of standards or (standards and practices), competitive forces influence their rulings. Moreover, the American public has accepted some change. They saw on live television real world programs, news programs, that included scenes and language, sexual and otherwise, that were unedited and explicit. All of these changes have been reflected in television advertising as well.

As a programmer I found this book full of memorable and important television history, unique in its inside look at battles that are long over. Reading this book also hit home that some of the conflicts over violence and the impact of programming on children, which began so long ago, are still troubling us today.

This book is part history, part memoir, and all of it will be fascinating to students of television and viewers who will come to understand for the first time the difficulties of controlling history's most powerful medium.

Preface

In my third year at Harvard Law School I took the Administrative Law Seminar, given by the late Louis Leventhal Jaffee, the first seminar at HLS that dealt with communications law. I analyzed the Federal Communications Commission's comparative hearings process for my third-year thesis. In a very complex case, I was critical of the degree of fairness and lack of certain public-interest considerations in the FCC's decision in granting the license. I considered myself a First Amendment advocate and a strict constructionist in the interpretations of free speech.

After graduation, I interviewed with the late Julie Brauner, vice president and general counsel for CBS, the leading network, and told him about my interest in public-interest advocacy. He passed on my application. At the suggestion of Milton Neaman, an assistant general counsel at CBS, who arranged an interview, I went to the west side of New York to try my luck at ABC, which was fighting for survival as it awaited FCC approval of a pending merger with United Paramount Theaters. The late Geraldine Zorbaugh, general counsel at ABC, and the late Robert Kintner took a chance on a young neophyte interested in the new media. The year was 1952.

I spent three years at ABC and rapidly advanced to become assistant director of business affairs. I authored the first package agreement with an outside producer in a deal with William Morris Agency, which represented Danny Thomas. It served as precedent for similar package contracts for years to come.

I left in 1955 to join the CBS Business Affairs department; several years later, I became assistant to the president of the CBS Television Network, the late Louis Cowan, creator of *The $64,000 Question*. In 1960, after Cowan was dismissed by William Paley, I rejoined ABC under the leadership of the late Leonard Goldenson. The Paramount-ABC merger had been completed and approved by the FCC shortly before I left ABC in 1955.

Goldenson had just returned from an appearance before a congressional committee investigating payola, which was being examined simultaneously with the quiz show scandals. Leonard called me into his office and said that as administrative vice president of the ABC Television Network, I was to make certain he never suffered such a humiliation again. That gave me the role I would live with for the next thirty years when I became overseer of the Standards and Practices department, which replaced the Continuity Acceptance department.

With the economics of the industry changing, Frank Stanton declared for CBS and, in effect, the other networks that "we would become masters of our house." The networks would wrest control and program production from the advertising agencies, which meant Standards and Practices would assume responsibility and greater control over what went on the air. The mandate included supervision of the quiz shows to maintain their integrity and the responsibility to review all entertainment programming for taste, truthfulness, and appropriateness for broadcast.

Within a short time, the department faced its most trying work: questions about the effect of violence in television programs upon children's behavior and the explicitness of sexual depictions. I became the judge and jury for the radio and television networks and the owned stations.

Soon station owners and operators, the general public, and the government demanded greater care in program review. The industry gave the National Association of Broadcasters Code Authority oversight of entertainment programming and delegated certain segments of review jurisdiction to the Television Code Review Board. The board consisted of representatives of the three networks and six station owners or managers. It created code provisions and administered various aspects of the Family Viewing Hour policies developed in the 1970s. I became the senior member of the Code Review Board in the early 1970s and remained so until its demise in the 1980s.

This book is not about me, but about my experiences in the balancing of interests in an era of change. It chronicles the era in which viewer tastes expanded, innovative programs brought formerly tabooed subjects into the home, and special interest advocates became forces in the shaping of the debate. This book is about the battles, controversies, and decisions that affected entertainment programs during those three decades. In many ways, those formative years altered the way in which we perceived the world around us. This chronicle is also a portrait of a phase of pop culture and is a commentary on attitudes and the sociology of the times. Except for those of my peers at the other two networks, my experiences were unique.

I lived a life of paradoxes. Trained as a lawyer, intellectually committed to the First Amendment, an advocate of public-interest considerations, I found myself in the incongruous position of being the "censor." To accommodate the dichotomy, I set a standard for myself. As part of a com-

mercial broadcasting company, to which I owed allegiance and my financial well-being, I had to balance commercial realities with my principles
about constitutional concerns. I hope this book gives some insight into the
process that evolved.

The second vector of this book has to do with change. The thirty years
from 1960 to 1990 saw major sea changes in the tastes and acceptability of
entertainment material. The chapters try to capture some of that change
without my assuming the role of analytical sociologist, which I am not.
Some of the controversial matters, such as violent portrayals, sexual explicitness, and mixing of fact and fiction, remain with us to this day and
probably always will. To deal with some of the problems I faced, I wrote a
credo early on to guide me in this vocation. I have included it in the final
chapter. It stood me in good stead during my years as chief censor for the
American Broadcasting Companies.

There are many to thank.

In Broadcast Standards and Practices (BS&P): I could not have succeeded as vice president for policy and standards without the outstanding
contributions of those in the trenches who fought the daily battles and did
the initial screenings. They are: the "matriarchs" of the department, the late
Grace Johnson and Dorothy Brown; Tom Kersey and Bret White, who came
young and wet behind the ears to mature into a giant in the field; Robin
Graham, without whom many, many theatrical motion pictures would not
have seen the light of day; Dr. Alan Wurtzel, who led the department with
patience and fortitude and dealt with me and the production community
with finesse, intuition, compromise, and decisiveness; Harvey Dzodin,
who handled commercial clearances diplomatically and fairly; Julie
Hoover and Rick Gitter, Alan's predecessors, both of whom lived through
many a trying day establishing precedents where there were none; and I
could not have survived without the constant aid and assistance of the late
Joan Honan, Desiree Gayle, and, on the West Coast, Linda Haskell.

My bosses: the late Leonard Goldenson and Fred Pierce and the late
Elton Rule supported me and gave me the authority to operate in this difficult arena; and the late Si Siegel chose me as his assistant and taught me
brinkmanship.

Two special people: Andre de Szekely, the masterful editing genius,
who got me out of many an insoluble confrontation; and Susan Futterman,
who contributed more to an understanding of appropriate fare for children's television than anyone else I have ever known.

Producers: Aaron Spelling and E. Duke Vincent; Gary Marshall and

Leonard Hill; and Jerry Eisenberg, all of whom were warriors but understood I had a job to do and played fair in our negotiations. Barnie Rosensweig and Susan Harris, Paul Witt and Tony Thomas, who challenged and persuaded; David Wolper, the consummate debater over fact and fiction; Dan Curtis, who made me take back the "never" from full frontal nudity and with good reason.

My colleagues at ABC programming: Freddie Silverman and Brandon Stoddard; Tony Thomopoulous and Lou Erlicht; Esther Shapiro, Stu Samuels, Mike Eisner, and Barry Diller; Ed Sherick, Marty Starger, Dennis Doty, Lennie Goldberg; and Danny Melnick—the creative programmers and able administrators who fought and compromised and fought.

I owe a special thanks to Dr. Mel Heller, who guided me, counseled me, held my hand, testified with me, and applied a combination of forensic medicine, psychiatry, and good common sense to the many vexing problems. We missed having the caring and nurturing voice of the late Sam Polsky, who left us early on.

Thanks to Professor Lorna and Dr. Philip Sarrel of Yale University, kind, understanding and creative, for making major contributions to our comprehension of sexuality and how to portray it.

Mary Ellen McEvily was an insightful commentator on a rough draft and encouraged me to go forward, as did Dr. Robert Seely. Of course, my coauthor, Kaye Pullen, is a friend, a counselor, and writer, without whom this work would not have seen the light of day. My thanks also to Prof. David Marc, who saw the potential of this work, to Amy Farranto for her editorial assistance, to Sidney Liebowitz for sage counsel pro bono, and to Michael Ryan for his review and incisive comments.

I am most grateful to Michael Dann for writing the foreword. He is a legend in the television industry and a most creative program executive.

Lastly, thanks and love to my dear wife, Jane, who never failed me at many a stressful moment and has tolerated and supported me from day one, and to my wonderful children, Lee, Jeff, and Elizabeth, who gave me love and respect and made all this worthwhile.

The
GATEKEEPER

Overview

It is nevertheless often true that one man's vulgarity is another's lyric.

Justice John Marshall Harlan,
Cohen v. Calif., 1971

Democracy means the power to choose and choice is an illusion without information.

Lui Binyan

During thirty years of tumultuous social and political change, I was chief censor of entertainment programming for the American Broadcasting Company. From 1960 to 1990, as one of three independent, competitive gatekeepers, my decisions shaped the texture and taste of television programs that eventually reached 90 million homes. In this retrospective of the battles, occasionally waged frame by frame, over program content, I trace the evolving, sometimes accelerating changes in our national life as reflected on the television screen.

What was once sexually daring is now prosaic, and yesterday's blood and gore is now tame, but even in today's freewheeling media environment, familiar issues, with which I once grappled, remain in play: Does violence on the screen, large or small, breed real-life violence? Should children be protected from the influence of the media? And if so, how? Which demands from special-interests groups are valid? What is the role of the censor in a free society?

In the invisible but unique role I played behind the stage in television, I answered such questions in different ways at different times. This book is the inside story of my experiences as censor in what often seemed a quixotic quest to maintain an appropriate equilibrium for television entertainment programming as new social and political issues, such as civil rights, feminism, homosexuality, euthanasia, and sexual abuse, emerged. The pace of social and political change was also matched by changes in the

1

media marketplace as the dominant three networks faded into the multi-channel media universe.

The tensions in this ongoing drama were not only between the producers of programming and the networks with all the attendant economic pressures, but were also from the forces brought to bear by government, industry watchdogs, the public, and a chorus of special-interest groups. This book details the "backstairs" cast of characters and their conflicting needs and demands, but unlike insider stories of other corporations, this one deals with the images, ideas, and fantasies that dominated the public airwaves: a diary of our lives.

It begins in the late 1950s when scandals erupted over quiz shows and payola. When the public learned that those sweating contestants on such television game shows as *Twenty-One* and *The $64,000 Challenge* had received the answers in advance, an uproar ensued. The other deception primarily involved disc jockeys who accepted payment to play records instead of selections based on sales records or merit.

When the government and public attention came to bear on network executives, they reshaped the industry in ways that directly affected my future. In January 1960, after a brief stint at CBS, I returned to ABC Television Network as vice president of administration. One of my first mandates from an unhappy Leonard Goldenson, president of ABC, was to see that he never again suffer the embarrassment of having to defend himself before a congressional investigating committee.

Goldenson had been called to testify about ABC's relationship with Dick Clark and Clark's receiving money from an airline in exchange for an on-air mention. At the time, there was no legal requirement for such disclosure, but in the climate of scandal it came to be looked upon as another form of deceiving the public.

In the unhappy glare of public and government criticism, each of the networks, ABC, CBS, and NBC, took direct control over entertainment programming and expanded their departments of standards and practices. From that point on, every script, every program, live, film, or tape, was to be scrutinized by an editor for taste, accuracy, violent portrayals, and sexual overtones. This far-reaching review did not apply to news, documentaries, or sports, where the traditional rules of journalism governed. Eventually, that strange mixture of fact and fiction, the docudrama, would create a new programming category, which required the adoption of some of the news department's practices and guidelines.

The network's censorship of entertainment programming began in one of the most tumultuous decades of social change in American history. Political debates took to the streets, and the pattern of family life began to shift in ways that continue to reverberate. Innovation, experimentation, and exploration were the buzzwords in television programming as the adolescent medium grew up along with the nation. Television itself became the lightning rod for many controversies about what was happening in society.

Was television a "vast wasteland" corrupting the values of the young? How did television affect children's behavior, their attitudes, their reading scores, their perception of the world around them? The underlying question—what was the medium doing to us?—is asked about any medium, but with television and its intimate reach into the home, it took on a new urgency.

In the 1960s, Congress began to hold hearings on the effects of television violence and a substantial part of my thirty years at ABC was spent worrying about how to treat violence. To me, it's ironic that while opinion leaders, members of congress, educators, sociologists, and children's advocates intensely debated and tried to determine cause and effects of depictions of violence, the viewing public largely remained untroubled. Regional differences did appear on violence as well as other issues, but the gap between what the viewers watched and the opinion leaders debated created a territory where producers gained important leverage.

The public might have been blasé, but government officials in a continuing series of hearings and other pressure-making initiatives shaped the public debate and the headlines, and raised concerns within the industry. The chapter on violence provides an eyewitness view of the Dodd-Pastore congressional hearings, which ran clips of violence excerpted from action programs on all three networks. Is this a responsible use of the nation's airwaves? was the critical question posed to the government-regulated broadcasting industry.

The late Sen. John O. Pastore asked, "Even if only one child is affected by watching violence on television, don't you think you have a responsibility to do something?"

The government, broadcasting's landlord, so to speak, raised issues in the public forum, and, inside the house, the battles began with the producers. Programs such as *The Untouchables, Combat,* and *Mod Squad* all required tough negotiations to retain the action format but decrease the body count.

To give a flavor of this sustained, unremitting debate over appropriate violence, I recall two hours in a room with producer David Wolper and Brandon Stoddard, program executive in charge of ABC miniseries, counting the number of lashes in the whipping of Kunta Kinte in *Roots* and raising questions about how many scenes in an hour could contain violence in *The Mod Squad* or *The Rookies,* and if humor mitigated the impact of violence. How should slow motion be used? Would slow motion footage make *The Six Million Dollar Man* acceptable for 8 P.M. on Sunday?

ABC, CBS, and NBC each set up social research departments and conducted independent research on the effects of television violence on the child viewer. We were called to testify almost every year from 1962 to 1972. The battle to entertain, to capture an audience, to portray conflict, and to eliminate gratuitous and excessive violence was joined. It culminated in the ill-fated Family Viewing Hour.

The noisy debate over violence often was drowned out by equally vociferous complaints about the portrayal of sexuality, which I discuss in chapter 3. Congress and other public voices blamed television for sexual promiscuity, the breakdown of the family, premarital sex, and adultery.

While the 1960s roared on with increasing sexual permissiveness, our BS&P editors had to contend with the strange American dichotomy between what's acceptable in private behavior but not to be acknowledged or depicted on the television screen. The sexual times indeed were changing, but how much of that was "appropriate" in entertainment programming? Many a call by editors related in the chapter 3 could be designated arbitrary and capricious, and many once "controversial" topics are today's routine programming fare. In the late 1960s and early 1970s, television began to treat such topics as adultery, premarital sex, pregnancy (at first without use of the word), and abortion, but not without sometimes protracted negotiations about the actual presentation. Chapter 3 provides an industrywide view of the turning points in social change, as reflected in television programming.

Year by year, program by program, in comedy and drama, television programming ventured into more and more controversial and sensitive subjects in the arena of sex. Often, a theatrical movie or a made-for-television movie would push the limits of acceptable content or language. Series programming would follow and similarly push the envelope. At other times, a drama such as *Something About Amelia*, with its theme of father/daughter incest, was developed especially for television. For that 1983 broadcast, ABC provided a caller "help" line.

Besides having nitty-gritty battles with producers, I was asked to explain or defend my decisions as the censor to the network's affiliates or before industry panels. An important part of my role was to listen and learn from public and industry debates to frame a flexible standards and practices policy, but my bottom line was: the realities of commercial broadcasting. Working in a highly competitive industry, my objective was to keep entertainment programming responsive to change without forcing unwanted change on the viewers. The attainment of the objective was often subject to circumstance, the times, and several conflicting factors. Was I to be a conduit of viewer reaction or of advertiser desire or of special-interest advocacy, or was I to be the opinion maker? Could I free myself from the will of commercial and governmental interests and truly be the conscience of the corporation? How does one reach reasonable and valid decisions for a new medium where few knew what would succeed, let alone determine what would be acceptable program fare reaching into the private living rooms of America? "Censor" was a dirty word to those First Amendment devotees, but it was a mandatory function for those who saw evil in the forces of the controllers of content in this new medium. My role as censor developed and changed along with the substance and style of entertainment programming during thirty years.

Perhaps "gatekeeper" better describes the function of the television censor. When new doors are opened, and taboos broken, the censor holds the key to standards of entry or passage. There are no better illustrations of the dynamics of change than the confrontation we had with Woody Allen when ABC purchased his motion picture *Annie Hall*, or the caustic sessions with the late Richard Brooks over edits in his *Looking for Mr. Goodbar*, which occasioned a change in a long-standing policy of requiring the MPAA to review our edits and rerate R pictures.

After editing *The Last Picture Show*, in the fall of 1974 on a Moviola on a back lot in Los Angeles, with Peter Bogdanovich on one side and Andre de Szekely, our creative editor, on the other, I vowed I would never again subject myself to such tension and stress. Bogdanovich resisted our editors' cuts, and the only solution was to sit and negotiate frame by frame our cuts and his reluctance. Editing theatrical movies for television, as chapter 4 details, was a chore that cable never faced and today's broadcaster finds less of a burden.

Is it strange or hypocritical to mention freedom of expression in the same breath with censorship? Maybe, but censorship in television sometimes creates strange alliances. Often, our role was to try to see how to help get the program on the air rather than just say no.

Probably a turning point in both television acceptability of program content and the audiences awakening to a hidden problem in our society was a movie of the week, *Something About Amelia*, the story of father/daughter incest. Producer Leonard Goldberg convinced Brandon Stoddard in ABC Programming that he could deliver a movie within acceptable boundaries. Goldberg and I found the way. Movies of the week, MOWs, were introduced by Barry Diller early in his career in the programming department.

Motion pictures originally produced for theatrical presentation were becoming more expensive, as each network bid higher license fees for top product. Barry created the ninety-minute movie as an economic and entertaining substitute, and promoted it as he would a motion picture bought for television viewing. He sought provocative and controversial subjects that broke down barriers to topics and treatment.

For example, *That Certain Summer* was the first full-length television drama about homosexuality. The story behind that groundbreaking drama is told in chapter 5. The movie won critical acclaim and distinguished the movie of the week as a hit weekly series.

High on the BS&P agenda were programs designed for children. One of the motivators and leaders in the battle for programs designed for children was Peggy Charren. The founder of Action for Children's Television (ACT), she focused her attention, and ours, on when was television going to give children the healthy, educational, "pro-social," entertaining programs its public-interest responsibility dictated. Chapter 6 relates the efforts ABC made to address that question.

Saturday morning, weekday, and programming designed primarily for children and teenagers became the target. In the mid 1970s, the term "pro-social" set a standard for program content in these categories.

Academic researchers, the PTA, and the baby boomers of the 1950s who were beginning to raise their own families took interest. The responsibility of the media, they said, was not only to ensure that children were not harmed, but also to help children develop skills and values conducive to positive mental growth. Children's programs should deal with sex roles, role modeling, ethnicity, and stereotyping.

All this "goodness" and conscience, however, had to be placed within the framework of a commercial broadcasting system governed by the economics of free enterprise. We could not just educate. We had to educate, entertain, and sell.

Of prime concern, then as now, was the effect of Saturday morning cartoons. Not until the late 1960s were animated cartoons created primarily for television. Earlier cartoons were made for theatrical distribution and catered to both an adult and child audience. Filled with violent action, stereotypes, white- and male-oriented, they became the subjects of critical disdain, and various writings espoused their behavioral harm on young minds. A controversy emerged between those who argued violence is violence in whatever form and those who excepted comedic violence from the potentially harmful category.

Michael Eisner, now chairman of Walt Disney, then head of Saturday morning children's programs at ABC, came to the office to seek acceptance of the new *Superfriends,* a version of Superman and Batman in action-adventure cartoons. Was *Superfriends* an opportunity to affect a child's perception of sex roles and role modeling? You bet it was! *Superfriends* would introduce the first woman superhero, Wonder Woman, along with black, Asian, and Indian superheroes as role models.

In 1972, ABC began an afternoon series of one-hour specials that reached deeply into the quality of life for young teenagers. All the programs in *The ABC Afterschool Specials* had one goal: to respect the needs, intelligence, and sensitivity of children.

Throughout these several decades, there were conscious efforts to meet the intelligent and valid criticism of programs for children. It was an enlightened era in which we sought to brighten the horizon of young people.

To participate in change, as I often witnessed, requires courage and stamina. Frequently, television was the scapegoat and was sometimes simply caught in the cross fire of cultural wars. The public, elected officials, individual station operators and management, and the advertising community all looked to the networks to meet and answer the frustrations of the time.

Stop destroying the moral fiber of the nation, some cried. Set standards to hold back the tide of change, others insisted. At the same time, the networks had to respond to the voracious appetite of viewers for new and diverse programs; most of these viewers seemed ready for changes in programming content. One facet of the censor's job became to serve as a gatekeeper of values and morals, as arbiter of good taste, as judge of fairness. The censor was to listen to the pleas of the conservative, religious, and cultural elite interests. On the other hand, he was not to turn away from the liberals, civil libertarians, feminists, and ethnic and social constituencies seeking similar opportunity to influence the viewer.

Chapter 7 reviews my experiences with the numerous special-interest advocates who wanted their voices heard on television or their point of view presented in programming. Returning from a short lunch one afternoon in the middle 1960s, I learned a homosexual activist group had taken over Leonard Goldenson's office to protest an episode of *Marcus Welby, M.D.* This was the first of many clashes with the homosexual community. While most confrontations with special-interest advocates were not as dramatic, the necessity to listen and respond to divergent interests occupied much of my time and energy.

Television matured and so did viewers, who became more sophisticated not only in their viewing, but also in their tactics to get a response from the industry. Morality in Media held hearings about family values; the Reverend Donald Wildmon formed fund-raising groups to sustain attempted boycotts on advertisers who sponsored programs that they felt should not be telecast. This is also part of the story.

Besides my role at ABC, I served along with several station representatives, some affiliated with networks, others from independent stations, on the National Association of Broadcasters Television Code Review Board. Its function was to serve as the legislative and judicial body governing industry compliance with a code of principles and guidelines. The code was in addition to rules of permissible entertainment programming under which all the networks and some stations operated.

I became the Code Review Board's senior member in the mid 1970s and dominated its deliberations for the next twenty years. The Code Review Board meetings in the 1970s were scenes of rancorous debates about the Family Viewing Hour, which I chronicle in chapter 8.

The debacle over the Family Viewing Hour brought to a climax the debate on violence and sex on television. It also raised such questions as whether FCC commissioner Richard Wiley with his jawboning to the networks was doing for the government what it could not do by regulation. Were his conversations more cajoling or did they have the weight of "state action" and a violation of the First Amendment? Was it to benefit the health and welfare of our children or the beginning of government control of programming?

Not just the broadcasters battled this major initiate to change television programming by creation of a "no violence and no sex" zone; the Hollywood production community also rose up in arms. They believed that their First Amendment rights were being trampled upon to their creative (and, of course, their economic) detriment. Norman Lear and Danny Arnold, among others, led the charge and brought suit to reverse the policy and also sought damages. A court ruling that eventually found the Family Viewing Hour unconstitutional was reversed on appeal, and the issue remains an open question.

The debate, however, over violence in television programs and the government's role in pushing for industry reform continues today.

As I looked at how I approached the portrayal of violence, the expression of love and sex, and the intertwining of the breaking of taboos in this three-decade review, I realized that television is a diary of our lives. Television programming is ultimately the culture. Family values have been in constant clash with the pushing of the envelope, the opening of reality, and the press of exploration.

The censor's role in television program review is delicate. If television indeed defines our culture as it both reports and sets the agenda, the censor is in a position to temper its message or permit an accurate reflection of its realities. A news editor has to determine how many times the Zapruder film of President Kennedy's assassination should be run. How many times do we view excerpts of the beating of Rodney King? An entertainment editor has to determine how many programs can deal with child abuse or sexual harassment. How much violence is permissible? Should we show blood, decapitation, gore? Television acts out our conflicts and in doing so sometimes portrays our excesses. Television shows and applauds our sexuality while mirroring our behavior. How much skin do we show? Can two people—man and woman, man and man, woman and woman—be seen in bed together? Can they hold hands, can they "do it"?

Another major task of the censor involves the sensitive question of how to achieve balance. Unlike censors in other media, the television censor is the guardian of the public interest. The licensee, the owner or operator of a television station, owes his operating privilege to the public, but to run a successful business requires shareholder or private investment, advertiser support, and station distribution. Those dual realities, the government license and the economic enterprise nature of the business, put restraints on advocacy. The privilege carries the responsibility to preserve a sense of fairness and good taste in balancing diverse interests in the presentation of controversial issues. That is also the role of the gatekeeper.

The docudrama is a form of drama/storytelling invented by the entertainment divisions of the networks to portray real people and real events. This type of drama is fraught with the danger of misleading the viewer. Its success, however, depends on dramatic moments of shock, sensation, jeopardy, fear, and personal grief. The censor finds himself constantly in the middle of satisfying these conflicting options.

Because of television's unique capability of visually bringing timely news and entertainment into the home, clear distinctions had to be made between fact and fiction. Dealing with a movie about Mae West, where legendary tales were not that harmful to the subject's public personae, was much different from presenting the life story of Jackie Kennedy Onassis. That docudrama, prepared without her cooperation, had to meticulously follow the public record for legal reasons as well as those of credibility.

In programs such as *Baby M,* the surrogate mother case, the court transcript became the bible. In *Separate but Equal,* based on the landmark case *Brown vs. Board of Education,* an irate and furious George Stevens Jr. battled, for dramatic license, for scenes that we felt were incorrect. Former president Richard Nixon never forgave ABC for telecasting "Final Days."

The telling of real events about real people constantly created battles, as truth and accuracy clashed with creative license for storytelling, as will be seen in chapter 10. To serve the public locally as a community station operator takes a great deal of discrimination and judgment. To serve the public from a network point of view can be accomplished only by consensus.

The censor not only had the responsibility of being the conscience of the network and the arbiter of good taste, but he also had to answer to Congress on behalf of his company along with program and senior management.

The censor deals with certain givens. The medium is the message. The viewer believes what he sees, most of the time. Television's role is to entertain, to inform, to educate. Often it is difficult to distinguish one from the other. A license to broadcast is to operate in the public interest, convenience, and necessity. Often it is difficult to distinguish what is in the public interest and what is in the private, the advertiser, the advocates, or the creator's interest. So there is a censor—a gatekeeper.

"For better or for worse," Warren Burger, former chief justice of the Supreme Court, said,

> editing is what editors are for and editing is selection and choice of material. That editors—newspaper or broadcast—can and do abuse this power is beyond doubt, but that is not reason to deny the discretion [to the broadcaster] Congress provided. Calculated risks of abuse are taken in order to preserve higher values. The presence of these risks is nothing new, the authors of the Bill of Rights accepted the reality that these risks were evils for which there was no acceptable remedy other than a spirit of moderation and a sense of responsibility and civility on the part of those who exercise the guaranteed freedom of expression."[1]

To act responsibly, to preserve a sense of fairness and good taste, to respect the dignity of man, to balance interests that the medium serves, to permit the exploration of new ideas and examination of old practices— these were some of my objectives as gatekeeper, censor, editor, and manager of change. The role censorship plays in a free society is the subject of chapter 11.

Standards for programming changed during my thirty years as a network censor in response to the many twists and turns in our political and social lives. The following chapters detail how and when taboos were broken, which values fell, which survived, and which emerged. Together they tell the stories behind the stories that served as a diary of our lives.

Violence

In June 1961, with 55 million television sets in use in 88 percent of all homes, Sen. Thomas Dodd, chairman of the U.S. Senate Subcommittee to Investigate Juvenile Delinquency of the Committee on the Judiciary, initiated what would eventually turn into a twenty-year investigation that would try to establish the cause of crime and violence in society. Television action-adventure programming was considered a prime suspect, and the focus was on the impact of television programming on children.

On the huge screen in the hearing room, a fifteen-minute montage of car crashes, murders, and gunfire in television programs was shown first to the attentive audience, which included network executives, research experts, producers, educators, sociologists, and others summoned to testify.

The screening of excerpts of violent scenes from episodic television series, scenes taken out of context, trailers and promotional film, and teasers all played sequentially before the audience in that hearing room almost four decades ago. It was the prologue of the continuing controversy today over the impact of television violence on children's behavior.

In his opening remarks, Senator Dodd said that "serious concern was expressed before this committee regarding the possible negative influence of an alleged overemphasis of crime and violence, and brutality in the content of television programs being viewed by children in millions of American homes."[1]

Crime and violence were on the increase in major urban areas, and some citizens, members of the clergy, parents, PTA groups, sociologists, and experts in crime control charged that the excesses of brutality, violence, and sexual permissiveness shown on television contributed to the serious delinquency problem.

Although programs containing violent depiction, primarily in prime time when many children watched, increased from 16.6 percent of total programming time to 50.6 percent in a given week,[2] the amount of programming also increased. Network executives were targeted as fostering

11

increased violence by ordering more "violence" in action adventure programming.

Programs that would appear remarkably tame today were targeted as too violent. Included were Westerns, (*Cheyenne, Gunsmoke, The Outlaws*); cop shows, (*The Untouchables, Naked City, Route 66*); and anthologies series, (*Adventures in Paradise, One Step Beyond, The Twilight Zone*). The cry was: Stop the violence! The battle line was not only drawn on psychological and behavioral grounds, but also on constitutional and policy issues.

Senator Dodd stated, "When decisions regarding the major portion of the broadcasts which enter each home are concentrated in the hands of a few men at the head of each network, then we rightly look to their decisions and ask how well the public interest, which broadcasters are under duty to serve under the Federal Communications Act, is being served by a program schedule overloaded with 'crime and violence.'"[3]

In response, network officials repeatedly expressed their concerns and fears that such inquiries about programming practices would endanger the exercise of First Amendment freedoms. Senator Dodd recognized the dilemma while quoting the late Dr. Joseph Klapper, a research scientist in mass media; "If depictions of crime and violence have an unhealthy effect upon even one percent of the nation's children, it becomes socially important to inquire whether and how the situation can be rectified. Dodd said "it is to this question that we turn our efforts." He added, "However, we must be cognizant all the while of the significance and importance of our actions whenever we inquire into mass media. We must realize that whatever the medium we attempt to evaluate—be it newspaper, the radio, television, or any other medium, we are dealing with the fundamental question in our democratic society of freedom of speech."[4]

The niceties of debate aside, the congressional inquiries had real-life consequences. In January 1962, Oliver Treyz, president of ABC, lost his job after being called to explain why a *Bus Stop* episode got on the air. Tame by today's standards, *Bus Stop* epitomized the overload of crime and violence on television. In the first episode of this series, "A Lion Walks among Us," Fabian, a young male singer popular with young viewers, made his debut as Luke, a fast-talking, charming delinquent, accused of the brutal murder of a storekeeper. The prosecuting attorney's wife, an alcoholic, is the principal witness; her testimony eventually frees the young man, even though viewers had seen him commit the crime. A television code viewing report had indicated the need to edit portrayal of the murder, reduce use of a switchblade knife, and eliminate vulgar language and implied salaciousness in Luke's whisper to a young lady. The ending, a murder-suicide, violated a code prohibition.

The cross-examination of Treyz and other ABC management caused embarrassment and pointed the finger of failed responsibility at the broadcaster. Treyz had to go. Rules and guidelines had to be written; practices had to change.

Treyz was not the only executive to suffer under the scrutiny of the congressional hearings. After a grueling session over the content of an episode of *Breaking Point*, that dealt tangentially with homosexuality, Thomas Moore, then head of the program department at ABC, disappeared from his hotel room, roamed the streets of Washington for hours, and, in the early morning, transferred to another hotel, as if to rid himself of the punishment of trying to explain the realities of the highly competitive world of network television to a panel of Senators. ABC, the youngest and least financially secure of the broadcast networks, used action-adventure programming to draw young audiences.

In response to the public and government concerns about violence, the National Association of Broadcasters Television Code and Code Review Board (now defunct) struggled with the issue and promulgated standards. The Code Authority office began a monitoring system to review excessive and gratuitous violent depictions after the program had been telecast. All three networks fought prior review as a matter of principle against prior restraint and, considering the time element, negotiating changes, and meeting a schedule date for telecast, as economically unfeasible.

In 1964, again under the auspices of the Subcommittee to investigate juvenile delinquency, Senator Dodd held more hearings, and the same issue reappeared: television violence and its impact on the young. Statistically, the number of violent programs had increased, because many of the programs shown in the 1961–62 season were being syndicated and replayed on independent networks and stations.

It didn't matter that the networks had established some restrictive guidelines, because the old programming was back on the air. The subtle, or not so subtle, conclusion again was that irresponsible, profit-motivated television executives were leading our young to increased aggressive behavior.

Action-adventure programming was indeed in an up cycle, and producers were inching forward in the quantity and kind of violent depictions. Beginning with the assassination of President John F. Kennedy in November 1963 through the violence of 1968, including the assassinations of Dr. Martin Luther King and Robert Kennedy, much of the news of the decade, increasingly dominated by the war in Vietnam, was itself violent.

Despite the realities of the headlines, however, it became increasingly politically correct for government officials, supported by academic encouragement, to indict television programming as the "carrier." What was lacking was some substantial evidence—research that could prove television "caused" violent behavior.

The hearings scene shifted in 1969 to the Subcommittee on Communications of the Senate Committee on Commerce. This powerful committee had jurisdiction over the appointments and financial allocations for the Federal Communications Commission. The FCC granted licenses and renewals to the owners of television stations and set standards for ownership. The subcommittee was chaired by a domineering, resolute and forceful senator from Rhode Island, the late John O. Pastore. The Pastore hearings brought the controversy over television and violence to a new intensity.

Later that year, 1969, the National Commission on the Causes and Prevention of Violence, created in June of 1968 and headed by Dr. Milton Eisenhower, issued a statement that concluded that violence on television encouraged real violence especially among children of poor, dysfunctional families.

After the hearings he conducted, Senator Pastore wrote to the secretary of health, education and welfare requesting that he "direct the Surgeon General of the U.S. to appoint a committee of distinguished men and women from whatever professions and disciplines he deemed appropriate to conduct a study which would establish *insofar as possible* the effects, if any, violence on television has on children."[5]

The surgeon general's Scientific Advisory Committee on Television and Social Behavior received a grant of one million dollars to review the literature, commission studies, and then report back to Pastore. Dr. Eli Rubenstein, assistant director for Extramural Programs and Behavioral Sciences of the National Institute of Mental Health, was appointed vice chairman, and the surgeon general began to select twelve distinguished scientists to serve on the committee.

The selection process itself became controversial, because the broadcast industry was invited to consult in the development of the research and was permitted to register objections to individual nominees. Several renowned academics in social behavior, child psychiatry, communications, and psychology were omitted from the committee, while two network representatives, the late Dr. Joseph Klapper, director of social research, CBS, and Dr. Thomas Coffin, vice president in charge of research, NBC, were included.

ABC decided not to object to the nominees, nor did we put forth a candidate. Everett Erlick, general counsel of ABC, wisely advised that ABC would be better off being able to accept or reject the report if we were not involved and instead worked with the National Association of Broadcasters. I believed that advice would only put us in the position of having to accept whatever guidelines or recommendations might come forward without the ability to make our own independent evaluation. In the meantime, in February 1969, we decided to conduct our own studies to give us a basis to create guidelines for the production of programs with violence.

Judgment day came on March 23, 1972, when network executives were summoned to the cavernous Senate hearing room. Senator Pastore, the chairman, presided; the case was presented by the very able counsel Nick Zapple. The surgeon general and the Advisory Committee, led by Dr. Eli Rubenstein, were there to present the evidence.

Senator Pastore, a master of advocacy and prosecution, set the tone of the session. Quoting "an eminent psychiatrist writing on the subject of violence," he said, "If the mass media seduce only one child each year to unfeeling, violent attitudes, and this child influences yearly only one other child, who in turn affects only one other, there would be in 20 years, 1,048,575 violence prone people."[6] Using terms such as "highly complex subject," "thoroughly scrutinized," "vigorous examination," and "couched in conservative cautious terms," he led the surgeon general and members of the committee who testified to conclude that the television networks were culpable.

Despite the prosecutorial atmosphere of the hearings, the report itself came to more equivocal conclusions. The research found no positive effects of aggressive television, but that didn't concern the surgeon general, Jesse L. Steinfeld, who stated that his "professional response . . . is that the broadcasters should be put on notice. The. . . . report indicates that televised violence, indeed, does have an adverse effect on *certain* members of our society."

Here is what he said:

> While the committee report is carefully phrased and qualified in language acceptable to social scientists, it is clear to me that the causal relationship between televised violence and anti-social behavior is sufficient to warrant appropriate and immediate remedial action. The data on social phenomena such as television and violence and/or aggressive behavior will never be clear enough for all social scientists to agree on the formulation of a succinct statement of causality. But there comes a time when the data is sufficient to justify action. That time has come.[7]

With cautionary additions such as "anti-social behavior existed in our society long before television appeared" and "we must be careful not to make television programming the whipping boy for all of society's ills," Pastore goaded Steinfeld into calling for action.

Pastore: Now in very simple language, will you tell me if this report by the Advisory Committee contains *enough* evidence and states there is a casual effect?

Steinfeld: Yes, sir, Mr. Chairman, I think the Committee report contains sufficient data to justify action.

And what *did* the five-volume report state?

[T]he data, while not wholly consistent or conclusive, do indicate that a modest relationship exists between the viewing of violence and aggressive behavior. The correlational evidence from surveys is amenable to either of two interpretations: that the viewing of violence causes the aggressive behavior or that both the viewing and the aggression are joint products of some other common source. Several findings of survey studies can be cited to sustain the hypotheses that viewing of violent television has a causal relation to aggressive behavior though neither individually nor collectively are the findings conclusive. They could also be explained by operation of a "third variable" related to pre-existing conditions.

The experimental evidence does not suffer from the ambiguities that characterize the correlational data with regard to third variables, since children in the experiments are assigned in ways that attempt to control such variables. The experimental findings are weak in various other ways and not wholly consistent from one study to another. Nevertheless, they provide suggestive evidence in favor of the interpretation that viewing violence on television is conducive to an increase in aggressive behavior, although it must be emphasized that the causal sequence is very likely applicable only to some children who are predisposed in this direction.

Thus a preliminary and tentative indication of a causal relation between viewing violence on television and aggressive behavior: an indication that any such causal relation operates only on some children, who are predisposed to aggression, and in indication that it operates only in some environmental contexts.[8]

So, despite the conclusions of the report itself, Pastore had his victory and the finger of blame pointed straight toward broadcasters. The message was clear: the industry had to act. And that is precisely what happened.

At ABC our review procedures were enhanced and our staff increased. I felt we needed some reasonable basis for continuing programs that contained depictions of violence and violent behavior. What we needed were guidelines with some social and psychological direction and substance.

The industry's actions and reactions in 1972 were part of a continuing response that had begun in late September 1968, when representatives from the three television networks and the NAB research staff met with Dr.

Melvin Heller and Dr. Samuel Polsky of Temple University to work out a consulting arrangement to develop criteria to evaluate television material.

The goal was to enable standards and practices editors, the censors, to distinguish between "beneficial" (cathartic) violence and "noxious" (gratuitous) violence that might stimulate antisocial behavior. Before the publication of the surgeon general's report, the theory of "cathartic violence," the beneficial release of anger, aggression, and hostility as an antiviolent factor, was still considered viable.

The late Stockton Hellfrich, a former NBC continuity acceptance (the precursor of standards and practices) officer and then director of the NAB Code Authority, the all-industry censorship or "police" body, had come across some writings of Drs. Heller and Polsky and was aware of their work in forensic medicine.

Dr. Melvin Heller, trained in psychiatry at Yale medical, outgoing, witty, bright, and ambitious to enter this visible field, was a professor of psychiatry, director of the Division of Forensic Psychiatry, and codirector, Unit of Law and Psychiatry, at Temple University. The late Dr. Samuel Polsky, everyone's dad, analytical, expressive, and so perfectly complementary to Heller in style and character, was professor of law and medicine and director of the Institute of Law and Health Sciences and codirector of the Unit of Law and Psychiatry at Temple University. Well-known in their respective fields, knowledgeable about current research, clinically and academically experienced, they were well suited to provide guidance to the networks. They would eventually become of value during the Pastore hearings.

At ABC, in the late 1960s, we had not as yet decided we needed our own in-house social research staff, which CBS and NBC had. The ABC television network was still losing money and did not yet believe itself to be a full third network competitor, even though the world treated it as such.

I did, however, call upon Heller and Polsky to help us formulate some definitive guidelines in preparation for testimony before the Eisenhower Commission on Violence in 1968. We had general guidelines in place. We would prohibit the use of violence merely for the sake of violence. When a story line or plot development called for the use of force, it had to be reasonably related to plot development and character delineation, and the use of force as an appropriate means to an end was not to be emulated.

Our experts, Heller and Polsky, gave us some more tenets. They said that in reviewing the content of programs, a variety of factors had to be considered. These included the makeup of the television audience, where some 10 to 20 percent of the populace could be considered psychologically immature and unstable. With this group certain program material is "indigestible," which meant certain steps should be taken that could temper possible negative behavior.

For example, Heller and Polsky pointed out that humor and fantasy were effective "defusers" of violence. A program then on the air, *The Avengers*, used satire, humor, and wit to detoxify the violence. *Dark Shadows*, with its horror, jeopardy, and graphic fear, was made acceptable the more fantasy prevailed. The inclusion of commercials broke up the "noxious content" of programs such as *The Invaders*.

Of even greater importance was the inclusion of consequences. Showing the widow or orphan of the victim put violence in a negative context. Another important guideline was avoidance of demonstrations of "how" violence occurred with more emphasis on "who." Unique demonstrations were to be avoided; de-emphasize how to do it in favor of who did it.

The movie *The Collector* was used to illustrate the need to avoid sadistic and erotic material. I had taken the film home one Saturday evening and shown it to my wife and two boys, then twelve and ten (our six-year-old daughter was asleep), and a psychiatrist friend and his wife watched. The conclusion was: Don't show that film! I introduced a whole new lexicon of terms in the review process, such as avoiding "inuring effects" and "dehumanization of character." I also prescribed that retribution should be used in context with other human consequences.

At that point, ABC continued its search for young viewers and became the leader in carrying prime time action programs with such adventure and western programs as *Grants*, *The Outcasts*, *The Big Valley*, and *Will Sonnett*, and in mystery and suspense, *N.Y.P.D.*, *The Mod Squad*, *Felony Squad*, *The F.B.I.*, *The Avengers* and *To Catch A Thief*.[9] With this lineup, we knew we would be in the forefront of any congressional hearings, and we also acted in anticipation of the surgeon general's report.

In February 1970, we decided to take another step to enable us to manage programs with "violent" content with some sense of rationality and responsibility. We engaged Heller and Polsky to conduct independent clinical research on the effect of violent portrayals in television programs and children behavior. Engaging Heller and Polsky over a five-year period cost about a million dollars.

We also engaged Lieberman Research Inc. to conduct attitudinal studies with an electronic pounding platform, a device to measure pre and post changes in inclination toward aggression, for about the same cost. The Lieberman study involved ten thousand children eight to thirteen years of age, from a wide range of socioeconomic backgrounds, mostly white, some black and Puerto Rican. The participants were from New York, New Jersey, and Connecticut.

Heller and Polsky were advised to choose children who might be considered most vulnerable to televised violence, specifically, emotionally impaired children, children from broken homes, and youthful offenders imprisoned for crimes of violence. We felt if we dealt only with normal children we would be accused of stacking the deck. So we went for the vulnerable viewer.

These children and youthful offenders were shown cartoons and programs such as *The Flying Nun* with Sally Fields, containing minimal violence; *The F.B.I.*, containing moderate violence; and *Combat* and *Felony Squad*, containing maximal violence.

The research was to serve several purposes. We needed to give substance to our position when we had to testify before any congressional hearings. During the five years of research, we also kept Dr. Eli Rubenstein, vice chairman of the surgeon general's investigation, informed of our findings and progress.

Before the various hearings, tough, grueling practice sessions were conducted by Jim McKenna and his staff of Washington attorneys under the no-nonsense surveillance of Everett Erlick, general counsel of ABC. Erlick's mission was to see that top management did not get any of the blame or criticism for its drive to be competitive with the other two networks. Neither Erlick nor the top ABC executives wanted a repeat of the Treyz or Moore disasters. The designated sacrificial lamb would be the "gatekeeper," for failing to contain excessive violence in the production of programs.

For me and for the company, this approach made the research to set guidelines and standards important. We wanted research to guide the standards to ensure our appropriate handling of content and to have our armor ready for testimony.

It wasn't all about defense, however, because I also had an intellectual curiosity and a strong sense of ethics about the need to balance the commercial realities of television programming with our social responsibilities to the audience. In this atmosphere, I directed our efforts in an area new in the production of entertainment programs.

The playing field was changing both competitively and culturally. CBS shifted its programming direction from a focus on a rural audience to competition with ABC for the young urban adults, ages eighteen to forty-nine. Under Fred Silverman's direction, CBS introduced such programs as *All in the Family* and *Maude* and canceled programs such as *The Beverly Hillbillies*.

In the fall of 1971, the new three-hour rule took effect, which allowed the networks to program no more than three hours in prime time. ABC moved to shows most "relevant" to the young audience, programs such as

The Mod Squad and *The Rookies,* and developed movies of the week with adult themes.

Guidelines and standards, along with strong management support, gave Broadcast Standards and Practices, known not too affectionately to many as BS&P, a powerful weapon in the control of program content. The producers, including the Aaron Spellings, the Quinn Martins, and so on, would strive for new and inventive graphic displays and words for violence, but BS&P editors exercised a strong veto power. The review of program material for violent content, both as to its dramatic effect and its effect on the viewer, had never been examined in such depth before nor would it ever again be.

The volatile period of the late 1960s and early 1970s produced disruptive and unsettling social and political changes. Against this backdrop of civil rights marches, protests over Vietnam, the war itself and the growth of feminism, television dealt with competitive pressures and the glare of national attention over its role in this confusing stew of changing mores and morals.

The broadcasting industry was itself divided by conflicts over television programming. On the one hand, ABC, often referred to as the fourth network in a three-network universe, and its two well-established competitors depended upon their ability to attract a mass audience for advertisers. No viewers—no advertising dollars, no profits. In addition, the three networks competed among themselves for the strongest affiliate stations, and raids and trades were based on programming success. ABC especially suffered from its lack of parity in the number of affiliates. All of this meant television programmers and producers, feeling protected by the First Amendment and driven by competitive pressures, weren't that concerned about social issues or congressional pressure.

On the other hand, top management at all three networks and station owners were well aware of the realities of the FCC's review of ownership every three years (the period of the license now is eight years), especially in an era when special-interest groups were vocal and volatile in their complaints during license renewal. Station owners were eager to avoid a costly and lengthy battle to protect their valuable properties. These concerns meant attention had to be paid to research and social scientists to respond to public and governmental pressures about program content.

During this critical period of change and confrontation, both within and without the broadcasting industry, the research conducted for ABC by Heller and Polsky found a number of changes in attitudes, fantasy, and preoccupation with aggressive materials in response to exposure to violent television programs. Programs with more aggressive content produced more aggressive fantasies. Although they found no evidence that television played any part in motivating the subjects to perform criminal actions, some in the group of youthful offenders were consciously aware of acting out crime techniques they had previously seen "demonstrated on television."

Heller and Polsky concluded that although television viewing did not appear to have any causative relationships to the criminality or violent actions of youthful offenders, there were indications that television can affect the "style," or technique, of crimes they engaged in, providing a "format" or vehicle for the acting out of a crime. As Heller described it, one young man said he was not motivated to commit the crime by having watched a television program, but he learned "how to" inactivate the burglar alarm wires from watching television.

As an aside, yet pertinent to the question of increased violence, was a comment that the tendency for violent relationships in these children was found to be rooted in early-life formative relationships and actual experiences of frustration, pain, and deprivation, rather than an exposure to television-portrayed violence.

Despite the ambiguity in scientific empirical correlations, there was some evidence, and the pragmatic path was for the networks to do something. Although ABC could not eliminate action-adventure programs from our schedule, we could exercise a degree of care and limitation, which was part of my continuing mission.

In network program scheduling meetings, I constantly brought up the question of a diverse program schedule. What percentage of the twenty-five prime-time hours, before the fall of 1971, and twenty-two hours in the ensuing years, should be devoted to the genres of Western, action-adventure, detective/mystery? From 58 percent of ABC schedules in 1960, this action category fell to 32 percent in 1972, where it remained for the rest of that decade.

In the standards area, we decided in the late 1970s, and early 1980s that there had to be a more formal, objective, semiscientific method of reviewing television program content. We sought a social science methodology to apply to our policy-based decision making. Although we had the policy statements, we needed a tool to aid the editor in making subjective evaluations concerning violent content—a "measure" to help determine what to leave in and what to take out.

We wanted a system to identify, label, and code violent program content. Although a coding system did not eliminate the need for the editor to make specific judgment calls, it would help standardize the way in which program content was evaluated, provide program producers with more stable guidelines, and give a standard baseline against which individual programs or episodes could be measured.

Dr. Heller with the aid of Dr. Alan Wurtzel and, later, Dr. Guy Lometti, both ABC staffers then in the Social Research Department, developed the Incident Classification and Analysis Form (ICAF). The ICAF system was based on the fact that not all violence is the same, but varies depending upon the severity of the action and the context. The system analyzed (1) the type of violence, (a threat, assault, weapons assault, confinement, and so on), (2) the severity of the violence (no injury, minor injury, killing), (3) the victim and consequences of the violence, and (4) the overall context. Using these variables, in a weighted system of scoring, a number was produced that was measured against baseline scores for an episode, which enabled the editor to identify excessive and gratuitous violence. The system gave the editor a method for a more constructive analysis of the program acceptability.

Workshops were conducted for all BS&P editors to develop definitions, criteria, and experience. Training sessions were held that not only educated editors in the use of the system but also provided them with psychological and psychiatric examples of effect, viewer expectation, and perception. These actions were a product of the ongoing hearings conducted by various congressional committees during the years from 1972 to 1982.

The fall after Pastore's famous indictment, ABC was at the peak of its detective-action programming: *The Rookies, The Mod Squad, The Streets of San Francisco, The F.B.I.* and *Kung-Fu,* were all successful in their time periods. Admonitions from Senator Pastore and social research aside, these programs could not be canceled.

Our response at ABC and within the industry was to conduct further studies when feasible, but all three networks mounted spirited defenses about the excessive use of laboratory findings to blame television for any and all social ills, especially violence. Occasionally, a real-life incident would add a provocative impetus to the debate. I remember one incident most vividly.

On September 30, 1973, ABC ran *Fuzz,* starring Burt Reynolds, which had been shown nationwide in movie theaters. Produced with the cooperation of the Boston Police Department, the story primarily involved the pursuit of an extortionist by members of the city's eighty-seventh precinct. Within the film, two subthemes were treated: the entrapment of a rapist and an investigation of youths who doused derelicts with combustible fluids and set them on fire. Satire and comedy relief, mostly about the ineptness of the personnel assigned to the precinct, were interwoven into the story.

Under ABC's policies regarding gratuitous violence, objectionable language, and ethnic and racial disparagement, the department's two most experienced editors viewed and reviewed the film several times and directed twenty-nine deletions totaling 306 feet of film. *Fuzz* was carefully screened and edited to remove gratuitous violence. The only scene that depicted a burning was preserved, in an abbreviated form, to show that the villain had been punished for the murders and other criminal acts.

Two days after the film was shown on ABC television six youths in a suburb of Boston, after having beaten a young woman, reportedly a lesbian, burned her to death after forcing her to pour gasoline over herself. Although the criminals were never apprehended, nor was it ever established that the gang had seen the film, the police commissioner stated that the film might have contributed to the crime. In fact, from reports in the neighborhood, it appeared more like a vendetta against the white lesbian. The victim herself before her death told the police that the black youths had said to her that "they don't want any whites here."

The press reports of the crime were imprecise, and substantially inaccurate. The criticism of the film involved two scenes. In the first, a detective, dressed as a hobo, loiters in an alley to decoy the youths, who have reportedly burned various derelicts. The ploy works, and the detective is accosted by the suspects. In a series of three quick camera cuts, about five seconds, the detective is kicked, a match struck, almost imperceptibly, and the detective winds up in a pool of water. The only action in the scene involves the kick. If the derelict-burning theme had not been established in earlier dialogue, it would not have been possible to determine what happened, because the actual burning, fourteen seconds, had been edited out.

In the second incident, which occurred in the film's final scene, the extortionist, wounded by police gunfire, took refuge on a riverside dock. By chance, the two sadistic youths approach him, splash the inflammable liquid, and ignite it. On fire, the extortionist jumps in the river to extinguish the flames. The action in this scene covers about fifteen seconds, having been reduced from the original, which showed the extortionist aflame and screaming.

After the controversy, we rescreened the picture for Heller and Polsky and for Stockton Hellfrich of the NAB, although the movie had been found compliant with the NAB code. We followed suggestions made for additional editing before the movie was retelecast.

But *Fuzz* kept coming up in a number of hearings as an example of gratuitous violence that might have caused criminal activity. No mentions were made of the edits and our efforts to eliminate "excessive violence."

Another headline-grabbing case occurred one year later. This one went to court and caused NBC officials great consternation. On September 10, 1974, at 8 P.M., NBC broadcast the made-for-television movie *Born Innocent*. In the two-hour drama, female reformatory inmates assaulted a teenage girl sexually with a wooden rod.

Three days later, in San Francisco, four teenage girls made a similar assault with an empty beverage bottle on a young woman. They told police that they had seen the television drama and had imitated the "rape" scene. The mother of the abused woman went to court charging the network and station with "wanton careless and negligent acts," with "willfully and intentionally" broadcasting the drama at a time when impressionable minors could see it and with acting "maliciously" and in reckless disregard of its possible results.

After many years of litigation, the United States Supreme Court in 1982 refused to review the case and let stand a Ninth Circuit Court of Appeals decision. That decision cited *Brandenberg vs. Ohio*[10] that the First Amendment principle of freedom of speech could not be overcome by an act of force or violation of law unless such action is directed to inciting or producing imminent lawless action and likely to incite or produce such action. The "speech" must *intend* to produce and be likely to produce imminent disorder to establish liability. A lower-court decision also stated that the action was barred by the First Amendment and that the negligence cannot be invoked against a broadcaster.

The latter statement became a key argument in a debate I had with Ellis Rubin, counsel for Ronny Zamora. In another legal test of incitement by television, Ronny Zamora, a fifteen-year-old Florida boy charged with murder, defended himself by contending that years of watching television violence had made him "involuntarily intoxicated" and was the cause of his actions.

The jury found him guilty. If they had not done so, the resulting litigation would have been awesome. It would have set a precedent for a principle of surrogate responsibility in place of individual accountability as well as cast a severe freeze on creative freedom. Not only would television and radio have been subject to liability, but also newspapers and authors would be implicated if their fiction or fact were alleged to have induced one person to injure another.

Television, always a creature of changing trends and tastes in programming, decreased the number of programs with violent content in the middle 1970s, but the violence became more reality-based, more anxiety-ridden. Hal Hinson, in an article in the *Washington Post*, May 12, 1992, made this cogent comment.

In the late 60s and early 70s, there was a tidal shift in our national attitudes toward violence in movies. The "Gunsmoke" era good guys . . . bad guys . . . —with the bad guys dutifully, bloodlessly falling over dead—just wouldn't cut it anymore. Not with the footage from Vietnam and race riots on the evening news. Television-specifically, the major network news divisions set the agenda, and Hollywood [and I would add television] had to match it in kind and volume.

In the fall of 1975, ABC introduced *Starsky and Hutch* at 10 P.M. (which was moved to 9 P.M. in 1976), and later that season added *S.W.A.T.* and *Baretta*. These three programs attracted wide audiences and once again brought to center stage the debate as to the effect of violent portrayals on television and violence in society.

S.W.A.T., which stood for Special Weapons and Tactics, produced by Aaron Spelling and Len Goldberg, raised questions about the appropriate use of force, alternative measures to total firepower, and the implication of the use of shock troops in a police state. *Starsky and Hutch,* also out of Aaron Spelling's shop, played with some wit and humor, but also brought the level of firepower up as did the nonconformist antics of Robert Blake's *Baretta*. All came the season after the end of the long and bloody "living room" war in Vietnam, which had brought so much violence to television.

Congress, the FCC, and antiwar and antiviolence advocates in our country again pressed for some reform in television programming. The industry would respond with what was called the Family Viewing Hour, or Family Viewing Policy, which is a story for a later chapter.

From my front row view of these years of debate over violence, I've concluded that as long as our society produces crime, violence, and antisocial behavior, the news or our dramas will contain depictions of violence. Storytelling itself has always relied on conflict, mystery, and horror.

Violence is more pervasive and invasive in our entertainment than ever, and only occasionally does reality shock us into questioning the origins of real-life violence. To scapegoat the messenger for the ills of society, or for creative efforts to shock, suspend, frighten, enlighten, and entertain the audience, will not diminish the social factors that foster violence, but that said, I believe the gatekeeper function remains necessary in television programming.

In looking at the literature over that long expanse of time and change, my conclusion, based primarily on statistical correlations, is that "excessive" violence on television influences aggressive behavior in certain children under certain circumstances.

It is also the case, as Dr. George Gerbner, a noted and vocal critic of television violence, has pointed out, that there is a desensitizing factor for those who watch a great deal of television. Certain viewers—women, the elderly, minorities, and the poor—who are routinely depicted as victims in television programming are inclined to overestimate aggression-related dangers in their daily lives. Today, it has been generally accepted by the academic community that there is evidence that excessive violence on television leads to aggressive and violent behavior among children and teenagers.

Dr. Deborah Prothrow Stith of the Harvard School of Public Health expressed the view of the impact of television violence by stating, "I think that the impact of television violence is small on most of us, but it's quite large on some of us." and "I believe that it is a public health issue."

Dr. Dorothy Otnow Lewis, professor of psychiatry at New York University's School of Medicine, theorizes that "people who commit violence suffer from a combination of neuropsychiatric 'vulnerabilities': (manifested in specific learning disabilities, psychotic behavior, and/or abnormal electro encephalograms or actual epilepsy) in addition to having a history of severe abuse and/or family violence during childhood."[11]

Television, because of its unique place in the nation's living rooms, requires managers, programmers, producers, and editors to exercise a standard of reasonableness in programming content. A perfunctory rating system is not sufficient, nor is the installation of a V-chip.

The amount and frequency of violent material is within the control of the broadcaster or cable operator. The quality and depth of character portrayal and plot delineation is within the control of the creator and producer. The expression, graphically or verbally, is within the purview of the reviewer. What is excessive or gratuitous changes with the storytelling. Context, consequences, humor, direction, and performance all serve to determine how much is too much or how little is illusory.

Warnings, ratings, and disclosures are devices to prepare an audience, but the broadcaster/cablecaster must accept his/her role in society as a responsible purveyor of programming that comes into the home. Of equal importance in sharing the role are parents who must exercise their responsibility and judgment about the types of violent programming acceptable for a child's eyes. The more the media universe expands, the more complicated the task becomes, but it is no less urgent an issue now than it was four decades ago.

Sex

In a *New Yorker* cartoon in early 1998, one child asks another: "What's oral sex?" The other answers: "That's when you talk about it."

Whether it was talk or the depiction, even the suggestion of, sexual activity, created controversy as television programming slowly, or too rapidly for many viewers, responded to changes in sexual behavior in society. During these thirty years when I was a key player in the debate over how far was too far for television to go in "sex"—the code word for all intimate sexual portrayals or talk—I was often reminded of the words of Philip Slater from *Pursuit of Loneliness*, a book introduced to me by my then tenth grade son:

> Every generation of Americans since the first landing has imagined itself to be more permissive than the previous one.
>
> Part of the puritanical, materialistic, technological basis of our culture requires us to de-emphasize and restrict sexual activity so that one can devote his energy to work.
>
> This equation between locomotion and lack of gratification makes us think of holding a carrot in front of a donkey, or an animal on a treadmill. In both cases the constant output of energy by the animal depends upon the sought gratification being withheld. Once gratified, the animal would come to a halt, and further locomotion would have to wait upon adequate deprivation.
>
> We make things scarce in order to increase their value, which in turn makes people work harder for them. The idea that pleasure could be an end in itself is so startling and so threatening to the structure of our society that the mere possibility is denied.[1]

Whether the reaction was based on as sophisticated a concept as that described by Slater, basic discomfort with public displays and discussions of private sexual behavior, or, as in many parts of the country, religious taboos, the question of sex in television programming became a constant source of conflict in the late 1960s and early 1970s.

The conflict became even more agitated and complex when a program mixed sex and violence, for example, rape. Slater made another pertinent observation in citing a Lenny Bruce sarcasm:

> Critics of censorship are fond of pointing out that censors are strangely tolerant of violence—that it is perfectly all right for a man to shoot, knife, strangle, beat, or kick a woman so long as he doesn't make love to her.
>
> Lenny Bruce used to point out that a naked body was permissible in the mass media as long as it was mutilated. This is true, but for a very good reason: our society needs killers from time to time—it does not need lovers.[2]

If the older generations were queasy and uneasy with the "youth quake" that rocked society, the young who shattered conventions in behavior and conversation were ready for television to respond to the new social landscape. The late Oliver Treyz, the brilliant, erratic, undisciplined salesman-researcher, marketer, and innovator, recognized the receptivity of younger viewers to change and sought that audience to drive the American Broadcasting Company's prime-time emergence as a national network in the 1960s.

Leonard Goldenson's canny awareness of audience desires and his motion picture company connections also helped develop the concept of counterprogramming, going for that "other" audience, the younger demographic, the eighteen to forty-nine year-olds. Leonard had a keen business sense and an intuitive feel for what the audience might like to watch. He was a showman out of the old school with modern-day vision. Brought up in a small rural community in Pennsylvania and educated at Harvard, he could take the pulse of middle America as well as the wishes of sophisticated urban New Yorkers. Not only did he bring original theatrical motion pictures to television as a new source of program supply, but he pursuaded the motion picture companies to bring their vast production capabilities to television programming. These producers also brought their experience with a more liberated approach to sexuality and violence, because motion pictures generally ran five to ten years ahead of television programs in their explicitness.

Programs such as *Bus Stop, Naked City, The New Breed, Sunset Strip,* and *Maverick* began the era of more mature television programming. As previously discussed an episode on *Bus Stop* was the focus of the Dodd hearings in 1962. Now we look at that incident from the standpoint of sex.

Entitled "A Lion Walks among Us," this was the storyline:

An illiterate 19-year old boy, an attractive Jimmy Dean type, is on trial for murder in Sunrise. He's a charming delinquent, but obviously a sexual psychotic among other things, and is adored by teenage girls. The principal witness at the trial is the alcoholic wife of the deputy district attorney in Sunrise. It seems she gave the boy a ride into town and, according to the defense attorney, stopped along the way for a "little fun and games," thereby making it impossible for the accused to have been at the scene of the crime at the time the murder was committed. It is her testimony that eventually frees the young man, even though we have seen him commit the actual murder earlier in the story.

Once freed the boy is in need of money and he calmly robs and kills his own defense attorney. This cold blooded act became the point of contention as to gratuitous violence. Walking away from the scene of this crime, he is once again picked up by the same lady. She's been waiting for him and they drive off together. She and her husband have been embarrassed and humiliated by this delinquent, but this time she is determined that he will not ever again hurt or humiliate anyone again and coolly drives the car off a cliff killing both in a fiery coffin.[3]

The San Antonio affiliate, KONO-TV, refused to run the episode on the ground that it contained "sexual perversions, indiscriminate use of obscene language [*hell's* and *damn's*, and maybe a *bastard*] sexual immorality . . . [married woman–young man adultery]."

The Dodd hearings had influenced the three networks to make conscious efforts to reduce the portrayal of gratuitous violence in programming, but in the 1970s, sexual topics became more predominant. Dr. Heller raised the warning signal during a briefing session in 1972: "to the extent that you're successful in curing, limiting in some way, toning down violence, to that extent you will be inviting to fill that vacuum with increased emphasis on sex." He was right. The sexy seventies would see many barriers fall in television programming.

An article in the *New York Times*, November 4, 1973, noted:

but the idea of increased television permissiveness did not spring full grown from the brows of Lear and Yorkin [*All in the Family*], it was a symptom, an idea whose time would have come, even if Lear and Yorkin had been dentists instead of producers.

The most convincing and symbolic piece of evidence of the change in television morality was the revelation that Ozzie Nelson in his new show "Ozzie's Girls" had taken out a subscription to Playboy! If Rick or David had brought that into the Nelson household [in *Ozzie and Harriet*, the husband and wife slept, fully clothed, in separate beds] in the 50's all *HECK* would have broken loose.

These visible signs of change made affiliate station managers very nervous. To respond to these fears and keep pace with change, the NAB Code was amended to include in its preamble: "Encourage programs that are innovative . . . that deal with significant moral and social issues, that present challenging concepts that relate to the world in which the viewer lives."

In November 1973, not long after the purchase of the motion pictures *Midnight Cowboy, Klute, The Graduate,* and *The Last Picture Show,* I told the ABC affiliates that "topical program treatments dealing with interpersonal relationships, if presented in a thoughtful, concerned and non-exploitative manner, reflecting social issues existing in society, are proper television fare." I also emphasized our commitment not to be sensational, exploitative, or salacious, but to handle such topics with great care, honesty, and integrity.

It certainly was a balancing act then and in the years and programs ahead. *Marcus Welby, M.D.* took on pedophilia, pregnancy, and abortion. We ran such provocative theatrical movies as *Irma la Douce, Rosemary's Baby,* and *Bob & Carol & Ted & Alice.* The separate beds were gone, but no nudity. Not yet.

The affiliates were not happy, because they were on the front line in their communities. A committee of the Board of Governors from Dallas, Little Rock, Philadelphia, and Washington, D.C., wrote to the president of the ABC Television Network, in April 1973; "I'll not bore you with the 'knits and knots,' but there is one subject that I think absolutely must be number one on the list of concerns in the broadcast industry and that is the *permissiveness* that continues in radio and television."

A television dramatization of Eugene O'Neill's *Long Day's Journey into Night* came in for criticism for its use of graphic language and almost unbearable realism. The mixture of sex and violence exacerbated the controversy. I had to apologize for what was considered a particularly "exotic" lovemaking scene in an episode of *Toma,* an action detective series. In response to station complaints Dr. Heller wrote the following defense for this episode:

> A short comment is in order about the mildly erotic scene between Toma and his wife, in which the brief portrayal of their love-making is introduced. This scene is tastefully presented within today's standards and serves effectively to introduce elements of tenderness and passion in the marital relationship between an otherwise pugnacious young hero and his wife.

It is a brief intimate moment, well within the bounds of acceptable cinematic representation of normal heterosexuality, and underlines the fact that this detective is human, has a personal family life, *and loves some people very deeply.* This is in contrast to portrayals of detectives as tough bachelors who leer at secretaries or an assortment of pulchritudinous incidental female characters, and who are depicted as unattached, and belonging to no one in particular. Toma, commendably, is portrayed as a real person, with meaningful emotional involvements. His risks and dangers involve a wife and child, and he is thereby identified by the audience as a human being who is a detective, rather than as a "private eye" who sleeps on a cot in his office, and who makes impersonal love to a variety of casually encountered females living in plush luxury.

Series programming was troublesome, but my staff and I faced more difficult problems in editing motion pictures purchased for television. Peter Bogdanovich's *The Last Picture Show,* a critically acclaimed movie, starring Cybill Shepherd and Cloris Leachman, was scheduled for a Sunday night during the all-important November "sweeps" period, when the Nielsen ratings determine how much stations can charge for advertising time.

Bogdanovich was reluctant to edit any of the graphic sexual scenes, nudity, and dialogue. Barry Diller, then in charge of motion pictures for television and the movie of the week, knew he had to deal with the arrogant and brilliant director to get the potentially highly rated movie on the air. He asked me to meet with Peter to edit the film.

The meeting to negotiate an acceptable television version was arranged though the good offices of the premier ABC editor for motion pictures, Andre de Szekely. Andre was the best, a skillful editor, who retained the creative integrity of the original in making edits for television, and was respected within the creative community.

In my first encounter with a Moviola, where we labored frame by frame over the film, I could not have had a better or more knowledgeable colleague. This is not to say he was totally supportive of my requests for changes; his task was to find common ground. After some six or seven hours of viewing the several scenes in question, despite explosions of temper and ruffled feathers, a version edited for television emerged.

The picture ran in the fall of 1974, and a few weeks later, at a Board of Governors meeting of the affiliates, the station managers were in revolt. We tried to reassure them that thirty-two scenes were edited, nudity was eliminated, and the looping and/or deletion and redubbing of thirty-seven words had been accomplished. We had also run on-screen an advisory disclaimer: "This film deals with mature subject matter. Parental judgment and discretion are advised." (This was some two decades before the current rating system went into effect.)

The film, which was scheduled at 9 P.M. EST, had also been submitted and rerated by the MPAA from R to PG, and had been prescreened and approved by the director of the NAB Code Authority, which was unprecedented at the time. One week before the film aired, it was sent on a television closed circuit twice for all affiliates to view.

We also reviewed the film with outside consultants Heller and Polsky. In this same season *Midnight Cowboy, The Sex Symbol, Summer of '42, The Graduate* and *Klute,* were telecast. Mel Heller once again supplied the rationale for accepting the film: "We received your list of edits with reference to the above [*The Last Picture Show*] and compared them to those we might have made on viewing the uncut film, had that been our assignment. As for your indicated cuts and edits, these are indeed the very ones we would have suggested had we been standing at your elbow."

And further, "let us compare it with 'The Graduate' which dealt with adultery! For good measure, 'The Graduate' also threw in a somewhat blasphemous use of The Cross as a weapon to ward off Benjamin's pursuers, and as a bar to the church doors in aiding his escape."

Then, comparing the work of Mike Nichols, another highly acclaimed director, Heller wrote,

Nichols makes much use of humor and thrusts his characters forth in living color. Bogdanovich's portrayals are in the black and white "reality" of the era which also succeeds in setting a depressing tone for his film.

The poverty and emotional deprivations of the Texans by comparison, are all too real. In "The Graduate" nobody gets hurt. Mrs. Robinson's potential divorce may indeed be a mixed blessing, and certainly for the hero and his audience, love triumphs. In "The Last Picture Show," love loses, the fates are harsh and the audience must witness multiple tragedies.

The safest thing is to say, "No" to any doubtful television materials. *But standards and frontiers change in the arts and literature, and even television must test the waters from time to time.*

Obviously, this is a test to be sparingly used, but unless it is used from time to time we cannot tell whether the industry's standards and practices are getting out of phase too far or too fast compared with the rate of change in a society that is constantly developing its own standards of freedom as to what they are willing to see and hear in their own homes.

The Last Picture Show and the other sexually candid theatrical motion pictures that were telecast that season were part of the continuing wave of change washing over the television landscape.

Two years earlier, an equally provocative topic had been depicted in a two-hour made-for-television movie that presented, for the first time, and honest, sympathetic, non-stereotypical portrayal of a homosexual relationship.

In 1964, Senator Dodd at a hearing quoted from the ABC Code: "sex perversion as a theme or dialogue implying it may not be used." By 1972, our code at ABC had embraced the NAB Code Section 7. This provision removed the negative and merely indicated that "special sensitivity is necessary in the use of material relating to sex."

That Certain Summer was first offered to NBC, who turned it down. Levinson and Link who produced *Columbo* for NBC, brought the drama to Diller, who agreed to develop and produce *That Certain Summer,* starring Hal Holbrook. In this sensitive and emotional story, a teenage son confronts his father's decision to leave the boy's mother to live with another man.

The negotiations over how to "tell" the story were long and tough. Levinson and Link, bright, talented, and determined, would tolerate little interference with their creativity and attempts to restrict their freedom of expression, but they understood the commercial realities. The production would have to be cleared by the stations and supported by advertisers to get on the air.

The negotiations came down to one scene in a key portion of dialogue, which appeared at page 72, scene 166, in the script, where Doug (Hal Holbrook) talks to his son, Nick.

DOUG

You probably heard about it in the streets or in school. But that's just one side—put downs and jokes. (pause) *A lot of people—most people, I guess—think it's wrong. They say it's a sickness . . . they say it's something that has to be cured. Maybe they're right, I don't know . . . I do know that it isn't easy; if I had a choice it's not something I'd pick for myself . . . But it's the only way I can live.* (pause) Nick, Gary and I have a kind of marriage. We —

(Nick shies away, anguished.)

NICK
I don't want to talk about it!

DOUG
(persisting)
Nick, we love each other —
(But the boy is trying to move off. Doug grabs
him by the shoulders, swings him around.)

DOUG
Damnit, *look at me!*
(then, softer)
Does that change me completely?
Do I have two heads:
Nick . . . I'm still your father.
(Nick's face is expressionless. But there are tears
in his eyes. Doug is tormented by them.)

DOUG
Hey, come on. Please . . . don't cry.
(He releases Nick's shoulders. Gets to his feet.
Paces. Turns back.)

DOUG
If it means anything to you, I'm happier now
. . . I lied to myself for a long time. Why should I
lie to you?

The italicized words were "written" by Heller, Polsky, and me.

To this day Bill Link (his partner, Levinson, died) bemoans the day he gave in to those lines. In the spring of 1992, however, Link was quoted in *Television and Families,* the quarterly of the National Council for Families and Television: "So we developed the script there [ABC] and were very happy with the outcome. There were bomb threats from some ABC affiliates, because this was really the dark ages and most gay people were in the closet, fighting a very hostile society. It was amazing, when we think back that it got on the air."

The changes in television programming in the late 1960s and early 1970s were primarily in subject matter: adultery, homosexuality, premarital sexuality, pregnancy (at first without use of the word), suicide, euthanasia, abortion.

It was still *talk* about sex, not action, on *All in the Family* and *Maude* but *All in the Family* marked a major turning point in television programming. Not only did it deal with language and behavior, conservative and liberal, traditional and contemporary, but it also subtly and pointedly tackled political issues and ideas as well.

Laura Z. Hobson, author of a groundbreaking 1947 novel, *Gentleman's Agreement*, about anti-Semitism, engaged Norman Lear in a lengthy debate about whether Carroll O'Connor's racial and religious slurs and epithets reinforced bigotry. There was also controversy over Rob Reiner and Sally Struthers living together before marriage.

I had recommended against accepting the program when the pilot, originally a version of a British television series, *Till Death Do us Part*, was offered to ABC. Leonard Goldenson, chief executive officer and chairman of the board of ABC, and Elton Rule, chief operating officer and president, also did not think viewers were ready for such a harsh comedy. At first, the series did fare poorly with viewers, but it survived and made the way for more experimental comedies. *All in the Family* also was a lightning rod in the debacle known as the Family Viewing Hour, which will be discussed in a later chapter.

Norman Lear and I were respectful adversaries for many years, and we experienced more tense moments when ABC aired his *Hot l Baltimore*. This was a farcical half-hour situation comedy taking place in a hotel frequented and administered by a repertory company.

Conchata Ferrell got her start playing the role of a prostitute. There were also two middle-aged gay lovers in the cast, which engaged in Lear-style cutting-edge dialogue. It was a prologue to our upcoming battles regarding sexuality on television.

In the fall of 1976, *Charlie's Angels,* produced by Aaron Spelling, quickly became the most graphic example of sexual innuendo and titillation. Critics dubbed the program "tits and ass" and "jiggle TV." Although Aaron and the programmers looked at the lighthearted detective series as fantasy and tongue-in-cheek humor, some critics and viewers thought the show led to depravity and more degeneration of standards. Coast-to-coast conference calls and battles became a weekly tradition.

Only nine years later, *Moonlighting,* another lighthearted detective series, also kept us in constant dialogue with the producers, but by then the standards and viewers' expectations had changed dramatically. A near-intercourse love scene on the carpet between the dueling detectives played by Bruce Willis and Cybil Shepherd drew faint notice.

One stop along the journey from *Charlie's Angels* to *Moonlighting* was 1977's *Three's Company,* which portrayed a ménage à trois with sexual innuendo and low farce. It too drew fire as further erosion of standards, and applause for being "with it" in a changing pop culture.

Also, in 1977, there was *Soap* as groundbreaking in its own way as *All in the Family* had been in 1971. It was also a milestone for ABC in its emergence as a competitor equal to its two older rivals. *Soap* like other controversial, pioneering shows, roused the troops on both sides of the fence, those defending the status quo and those pushing for more "realistic" television fare.

It began for me at a luncheon in the elegant ABC dining room on the forty-first floor of corporate headquarters in New York. Susan Harris, producer, writer, and creator of *Soap*, Fred Silverman, then head of ABC programming; Julie Hoover, vice president for standards and practices, East Coast; and I sat down to write the "rule book" for the program, which pushed the envelope in sexual comedy on television.

To the delight of Harris and Silverman, the program was controversial before it aired. Would Billy Crystal, prime time's first openly gay character, glorify homosexuality? Help normalize it as the religious community feared? Or would his portrayal stereotype homosexuals as the gay community feared? What would be the impact of such a humorous depiction of sexual adventures? "Soap" did open wide the bedroom doors of situation comedy.

That summer, Kay Guardella's article in the *Daily News* quoted the three network censors. " 'Soap' will make our jobs tougher this year than any previous season," predicted Herminio Traviesas, vice president of Broadcast Standards for NBC. "It will polarize the television audience," exclaimed Van Gordon Sauter, CBS's chief censor. My retort: "It's well done and will be successful." (Later, during a David Susskind panel with Roy Valentine of the Southern Baptist Convention; Everett Parker of the United Church of Christ; and me, Sauter stated there is no "sex" per se on television; rather there's talk of sex, and he gave as illustration the debate on *Soap*.)

Gardella continued, "Whether 'Soap' will break new ground, and deal with subjects, including homosexuality, which Schneider insists are all out front, or whether it will be rejected angrily by the public is not the question. After widespread public protest about violence, does television need another public spotlight on it right now? This is the real question." (The Family Viewing Hour had been defeated by the court only some six months earlier).

In the article, Sauter was also quoted as saying,

> I don't think television has the right to carry the banner of social change or to condone new forms of social activity. I think our broadcast, be it

comedic or dramatic, has to be rooted in the reality of our society. This, however, is difficult to perceive because of diverse audiences out there. If you consider the diversity of educational achievement, social perception, religious convictions and economic status, it's difficult to establish the parameters of taste. People have different expectations from different shows and different networks.

In my response, I didn't agree fully with Sauter's view that the public doesn't want television to decide and I argued: "While you have to reflect society, you have to inch ahead, too. This is your responsibility." I stressed, of course, that ABC would not be condoning immorality in *Soap* and that we would be "in trouble if we did not handle immorality in such a way as to conform with the majority standards in the country."

My statement then obviously straddled that ever-confusing question of how much television helped shape those majority standards. Change with caution was my motto, but, without question, the series did deal with sexually delicate subjects, such as homosexuality, adultery, orgasm, and premarital relationships, that shaped social and moral attitudes. Although the subjects had by the late 1970s been part of television programming, the comedy series dealt with more of these subjects than any one show ever had before.

By this time, it had been recognized that television would or could address special "niche" audiences and still be successful. *Soap* was not intended as an all-family vehicle, structured or intended for all members of the family, but as responsible adult entertainment. Choice and selective viewing were now variables in deciding the programming mix.

The courage to experiment came from strength. Such a pioneering show would not have been possible without the power of the ABC prime-time schedule, on its way to number one, and the success of the 1976 Olympics telecast. Changes in prime-time ratings of ABC shows had been helped by the Family Viewing Hour, soon to disappear.

The wit and sparkling satire of the series came from Susan Harris, a quality writer, still in her thirties, and strong of character, who had worked for Norman Lear and contributed to the controversial script about Maude's abortion. Fred Silverman, ABC's gung-ho program chief, determined to present a breakthrough program, with the support of the creative community, did a full court press on the affiliates, on me, on management.

Silverman's prestige as a programmer and his attention to detail made the program happen and contributed to its ability to break new ground. This comedy/drama innovated with its larger-than-life frank treatment of a wide variety of controversial and adult sexual themes.

In the summer of 1977, even before *Soap* aired, a mass debate erupted on the appropriateness of showing this program on prime-time television. Somehow, the first script and the "bible" were circulated to the press before telecast. Premarital sex, adultery, impotence, homosexuality, transvestitism, transsexualism, religion, politics, war, and ethnic stereotyping and other aspects of race relations were all treated in that material. An outcry arose from the religious right and other special-interest groups.

Why did the voices of the special-interest groups sound so loud among the protests? Equality of women in the openness and discussion of their sexuality was new to television. An early episode had Corinne, her sister, and her mother sitting around the kitchen table making small talk, barbs, describing sexual encounters, orgasm, the joy and pleasures of having sex. During the discussion, for the first time on television we were to hear the historic lines "I don't think you're depressed, Ma, I think you're horny" and "If you weren't so horny we wouldn't be eating so much!"

This conversation took place a decade before *Thirty-something* made such discussion routine prime-time dialogue. At ABC Standards and Practices, we at first objected to that kitchen table "girl talk," but Harris, with Silverman's support, made a fair and honest argument: "Why not permit women to talk about their sexual experience? You permit men to say the very things you're asking us to delete." The lines remained in the episode.

Billy Crystal rose to stardom through his portrayal of Jodie, the homosexual son of Mary Campbell. Not only was Mary Campbell (Cathryn Damon), who was Jessica's sister (Katherine Helmond), afflicted with an impotent mate (Richard Mulligan), but Jodie longed to have a sex-change operation. The boy dressed up in Mary's clothes and preened before the mirror, trilling "There's nothing like a dame." That didn't upset his mother nearly so much as the realization that "he looks better in that gown than I do."

Whether that first script report, a script, and the series "bible," the outline of future script scenarios, was leaked as a publicity marketing ploy, or inadvertently as sometimes happens in Hollywood, the press had a field day. *Time* in its July 11, 1977, issue led off the television section with a story, "Is Prime Time Ready for Sex"?

The opening paragraph read: "Will young Jodie go through with his sex-change operation and marry a football player? Will Cousin Corinne continue bedding down the local tennis pro, despite hard-breathing competition from her mother? Will Father Flotsky modernize the Mass by substituting Oreo cookies for the traditional wafers? And will 'Soap,' the new ABC comedy that features all these characters, be a TV sensation this September?"

It continued,

> The show has become this year's lightning rod for controversy, real or contrived. . . . Religious groups have quickly created a dispute about material that has not yet even survived the ABC censors.
>
> Adds Al Antczak of the Roman Catholic newspaper *Tidings:* "The desecration of morality, and of the Catholic religion in particular, is an outrage that calls for protest in the strongest terms.
>
> Until the ABC censors got wind of it, the show's writers had plotted Father Flotsky's seduction in church by Corinne, then an exorcism for their baby.

Even before the first headline or special-interest group appeared, we knew this satire was going to be a major problem with affiliates and advertisers. I took the case to the objectors. I explained our guideline of exposition, not advocacy. If the treatment of the topic was descriptive and satirical, neither condoning nor condemning, but telling it like it was without the stereotyping or physical aspects of the relationship, the producers could go ahead.

For me this was a role reversal, the censor turned advocate, and that was shocking to some. What was the "censor" doing defending "offensive" material? Censorship took on new meaning. The role had evolved into arbiter, gatekeeper, and judge.

We had our work cut out for us from June to September. The homosexual community was outraged that we would permit stereotyping in dialogue and action, dress, and some mannerisms. The religious community was outraged that we were condoning the lifestyle and proselytizing. A no-win, win-win situation. Demands were being made for prescreening by homosexual and religious groups to protect their interests. We declined and resisted.

Prescreening by demand of special-interest groups, threatened and actual boycotts of networks or advertisers, and government edict are roads that lead to inhibition and the eventual destruction of the free flow of ideas. Choice in democracy withers under the "chilling effect of prior restraint." Whether or not a violation of the First Amendment is involved, there is no question that prior review by any special-interest group could have a negative effect on the creative process in entertainment. That would only lead to similar consequences in news, documentaries, and commentary. The matter strikes at the very heart and spirit of the Bill of Rights and the intent of the founding fathers when they drafted that document.

A formal statement was prepared for press and affiliates. It read,

"Soap" was selected for our Fall Program Schedule, because it is an exceptionally entertaining program. It is a sophisticated, adult farce that parodies suburban life and television's serialized dramas.

ABC's programming philosophy is to present a broadly diversified program schedule that responds to the interests of its total viewing audience. "Soap" is intended primarily for the adult portion of that audience. It is funny, superbly written, performed and executed. It draws its humor and its insight from the elaborately complex inter-relationships of its characters and their life-styles. It is obviously impossible for any program that spoofs and satirizes contemporary manners and mores to avoid controversy or to appeal to every viewer. 'Soap' will be subjected to rigorous review by ABC's Department of Broadcast Standards and Practices from script stage to final production to ensure that the program's portrayals avoid salacious material, or sensationalism. The same special attention will be given to all promotional materials associated with the program.

Meetings were held with affiliates, special-interest groups, gays, religious organizations, and others. We devised a disclaimer for the opening show scheduled for 9:30 P.M. EST, 8:30 CST, which read: "The following program is part of a continuing adult character comedy. Certain dialogue and situations may not be suitable for all members of the family." It was shortened for the third and subsequent episodes by substituting for the second sentence "Parental discretion is advised." All promotions were carefully scheduled and carried the last sentence, as did newspaper ads.

The on-air advisory remained for the first thirteen episodes. The series lasted three years before Susan Harris tired of it, and it became too costly. The tides shifted and uninhibited sexual talk became less amusing as the 1980s saw a rise in teenage pregnancy rates, the AIDS epidemic, and increased concern about sexual responsibility. But *Soap* had made its mark. It would be the forerunner of *thirty-something* as well as movies made especially for television that dealt with heretofore forbidden subjects.

Probably the most difficult theme that had not yet been dramatized in a full-length television presentation was incest. A television movie with Suzanne Pleshette had alluded to a possible incestuous relationship between a mother and son, but never a detailed account of a father-daughter sexual relationship.

In 1983, Len Goldberg, who had left Aaron Spelling to develop movies and movies for television on his own, brought Brandon Stoddard a story entitled *Something About Amelia*. Deborah Ahls, a former schoolteacher and producer for Len, had worked on the project for several years.

Goldberg described the genesis of *Something About Amelia* in answer to a question at a seminar, October 22, 1986, at the American Film Institute's Elton H. Rule Lecture Series in Telecommunications:

A woman who is the president of my company, Debra Ahls is her name, came in one morning and she said, "I think we should do a television movie about incest." I said, "I don't want to do a television movie about incest." She said, "Why?" I said, "Because you know that's a very small problem. It's relegated to the Ozark Mountains." She said, "Why don't you read this." She had put together a file of everything that had been written about incest. I read it and I was shocked. Just shocked by it. I said to her, "You're sure this is all true?" She said, "Yes. Unfortunately, it is all true." So I decided this was a subject that we had to do. When I brought it to the network, they said that they were not allowed to do incest on network television, that it was a taboo subject. But since I had a long relationship with ABC and the man in charge of Program Practices, Al Schneider, why don't I take a crack at him. Because they would love to do it, if I could get it approved.

So I called him and he asked me why I wanted to do it. I sent him all of the material that I had read. He thought about it and he said, "Okay, I know you, I trust you. I agree with you; it's an important subject to explore. But only under certain conditions. You have to hire a recognized authority in the field to work with our authorities to be sure we do this in a valid manner. I won't allow you to show incest on the screen. Worse yet, I won't allow you to see the father walk into the bedroom and close the door behind him, which is, I think, worse." I agreed with him totally. He said, "But if you can fashion a dramatic story without those scenes in it, you have my approval to go ahead." We thought about it and we came up with what became "Amelia," which is the impact on a family when incest is discovered. He approved it. The programming department people approved. We got Bill Hanley who wrote a magnificent screenplay. It took him a long time but he wrote a wonderful screenplay. We gave Randa Haines an opportunity to direct it. She had just directed a few "Hill Street's" and one PBS show that I saw and was wonderful. She was the right choice for the material. We were able to attract Glenn Close and Ted Danson and Roxanna Zall to be in it. It all worked perfectly. It was one of those dream projects that just went together very, very well. There was very little that had to be fixed, even in the editing process. Then I got a call when we finished the rough cut that Al Schneider wanted to see the film. They were all shaking. So we sent a cassette to New York. He called early the next morning and everybody gathered around. I picked up the phone and he said, "Len, it's Al. I saw 'Amelia' last night," I said, "Yeah?" He said, "Thank you," and hung up. So they had no cuts, no changes, no edits—nothing did they ask for. It went on the air and we got the response we got, which was the good news and the bad news. We never realized how widespread the problem was. It was just an enormous problem.

ABC had an 800 number for calls for "help," and they were numerous. Callers responded with emotional and personal relief and sought help for occurrences like those depicted in the program. Not only had ABC presented a quality effort, entertaining, informative, disturbing, award-winning (it won an Emmy for best motion picture for television in the 1984 season), but a public service was rendered, without sleaze, advocacy, or sensationalism.

As I participated in the expansion of the boundaries of what was appropriate and acceptable in television programming, I continued to believe certain barriers would forever remain in place. In 1982, in an interview with Bob Michaels of the *Palm Beach Post*, with finality I said, "We will not see full frontal nudity on network television in our lifetime." I should have known better. Times change and so do expectations—let alone final statements.

Six years later I retracted those words when ABC was the first network to show full frontal nudity. During the shocking death camp scenes in the epic *War and Remembrance*, produced by Dan Curtis from Herman Wouk's masterful book, men and women were shown being herded nude into the gas chamber and, later, their bodies dumped from huge wheelbarrows into open mass graves.

Curtis, Brandon Stoddard, and I viewed the film one long afternoon in a screening room in Los Angeles at the ABC Television Center. To have changed those scenes in any way would have diminished their impact and demeaned the truth of the moment. There was no way that I could let that happen. It was tragic, brutal, humiliating death, not nudity.

A year earlier, in June 1987, we viewed a pilot of what was to mark the beginning of what Mel Heller characterized as a "series that would touch upon subject matters of high importance—merely, the future of mankind as it might be influenced by the infant and early child development of the next generation of adults." *Thirtysomething* was the program.

Mel Heller, in his letter of review—it was standard procedure in the 1970s and 1980s to have an evaluation from our psychiatric consultant to outline possible trouble spots and pro-social aspects of a pending series—continued his "diagnosis" with some general comments and one specifically to infant nudity, which was another first:

> There is an additional, pro-social area of importance upon which this pilot focuses. This deals with the sexual yearnings, frustration and fatigue

which afflict so many passionate but pooped young married's "blessed" with child. The underlying respect with which the writers address the privilege of parenthood—and the powerful, pervasive bonding between parents and child—sort of sneaks up on you in the pilot, out of the fog of funny stuff.

Now, for a couple of Broadcast Standards ideas whose time may have come. This series might just become known—among its other prospective sources of fame—as the one which first helped American viewers develop a mature, utilitarian and casual attitude about infant nudity, breast feeding and even diaper changing.

Few things are more cute than an infant's backside, and perhaps it is time that viewers realized that the front is not so terrible either.

Thirtysomething was not without its battles between the producers and BS&P. Marshall Herskowitz was intent on pushing the envelope in the treatment of real-life baby boomer problems. Reflection of everyday issues, situations, and personal relationships on thirty-year-olds was of great interest to ABC's demographically young audience and the subject of drama, conflict, emotional trial and tribulation. Good television fare, but lots of uncharted waters to cross.

Marshall and his associate Ed Zwick would test us at our annual producers meetings with content plans. At one such session in 1989, he asked whether we would object to a gay couple appearing in bed together, perhaps even embracing and kissing. We had a two-hour movie on the life of Rock Hudson in the works and knew we would have difficulties with the portrayal of his homosexual relationships. Although television had brought homosexuality, incest, child abuse, rape, family violence, and AIDS into America's living rooms, we had not gotten to scenes of intimacy or physical expression of homosexual affection.

After much storm and drama, we said no to the kissing. Herskowitz asked, "Why not? Doesn't it happen? This is the nineties! Nothing salacious!" But we did say yes to two men in bed together, touching. In my view, the difference is exposition, not advocacy; reality, not arousal; matter of fact, not exacerbating. The scene was shot. ABC lost more than a million dollars of sponsorship because of advertiser "pull outs" from the program, but viewers' expectations had permitted us to allow much on *Thirtysomething* that would have been rejected on any other dramatic show five years earlier, scenes such as Hope (Mel Harris) and Michael (Ken Olin) having a bedroom discussion in which Michael says he'll "pull out," to prevent pregnancy, or Nancy rendering lines such as "It's times like these I miss smoking pot," or Hope dropping her diaphragm on the floor.

The ongoing negotiations between producers and the network did produce some other angry confrontations. A script has a line about advertisers "panicking" and pulling out of a broadcast. The West Coast office advised Marshall Herskowitz that we would edit the line if he did not take it out. Herskowitz wrote to Brett White, BS&P editor:

> We on "Thirtysomething" have direct evidence of sponsors panicking, i.e., the debacle that took place on the Monday night before Polly Draper's rear end almost aired.
>
> Panic in its larger sense is the only way to describe the current climate among advertisers, when there is no evidence whatever that their market positions are threatened by the so-called media watchdogs.
>
> The line is spoken by an unsympathetic character in context, in an advertising agency; is not sexist, racist, libelous, in bad taste, or in advocacy of any political position, and therefore is not within the purview of your organization. Your sole reason for demanding its deletion is an inferred belief that it will embarrass or anger advertisers, and I regard your insistence that we cut it to be an intrusion into the creative process.

My response:

> The problem with the opening scene of Polly Draper in the pool had nothing to do with an advertiser or advertisers. BS&P's editor received a call from an ABC Sales Coordinator who had seen a screening service report describing the scene as "nude swimming." He also received a call from a friend at MGM post production asking if BS&P had, in fact, approved this scene. This caused him to review his prior approval and to cause an edit to be made. The definition of "panic" speaks to "wild, extreme, sudden terror." I don't believe that was the case.
>
> Whether or not the current climate among advertisers is a result of the threatening of their market positions or their unwillingness to participate in controversy or the desire not to be subject to negative comment; that is their prerogative. To conclude, as you do, that their action whatever it may be, is "panic," is an editorial conclusion without substantiation.
>
> In defining those matters which are within our purview, you left out one word—accuracy. That is the only reason for seeking the substitution of the word. As I've mentioned to you many times, I am not concerned about embarrassment or anger, I am concerned about honesty and integrity.

We kissed and made up and panic was eliminated, but the reconciliation was momentary, as it most generally was between producers and censors. Resolution, then on to the next controversy. On a *Thirtysomething* episode that featured a New Year's Eve party, at midnight the men and women embraced, and, of course, the gay couple embrace and kiss. "But Marshall, we just lost one million dollars because they were in bed together. Is there any reason to believe that this will be acceptable because the bell tolled?" We edited again over Herskowitz's anger and frustration.

In the 1980s and 1990s, more walls crumbled. *Unspeakable Acts*, produced by Allan Landsberg and Linda Otto, dealt openly and frankly with child abuse and child molestation. The script was reviewed word by word and "penis" and "vagina" spewed forth from young mouths. *Twin Peaks* gave us graphic sex and violence, totally acceptable, but as we leave the twentieth century, violent behavior in society once again draws attention to the excesses of violent programming on television and the call for moderation.

This detailed description of the history of sexuality in television programming and the role of the censor in the expansion of acceptable television fare shows how quickly the daring and dangerous taboos disappear. The most important fact, however, is that the three major broadcast networks no longer dominate entertainment programming. Cable stations, more networks, and deregulation all contributed to the ever-expanding, unrestrained media atmosphere in the talk and action of sexuality.

From coverage of such events as the Clarence Thomas and Anita Hill hearings, the William Kennedy Smith alleged-rape trial, and the Clinton impeachment crisis on the daily talk shows to prime-time programming, no sexual topic is off-limits. Whether today's generation is more permissive in its conduct than the one before, it is no longer debatable that television programming is far more explicit and frank than any of us could have imagined even in the swinging 1960s. A dichotomy exists, however, between what is watched and what is considered appropriate fare. Over cocktails or coffee among the most established of the establishment, sexuality on television is often condemned as immoral or trashy, but programs with explicit content command significant audiences for the networks and cable. Historically, when interviewed the mass audience had always indicated a desire for more documentaries, but when presented, these worthy programs never raised an audience above the several-million mark. Entertainment is about what we really want to watch, and it changes as we change, whether we admit our tastes out loud or not.

Editing Theatrical Movies for Television

In 1964, ABC followed NBC's lead in the purchase and broadcast of movies originally produced for theatrical distribution, and these movies became an important element in television programming. A blockbuster picture in the days before VCR's and cable generally commanded a large television audience and high Neilsen ratings, sometimes strong enough to carry the entire week for the network.

In 1968, the MPAA Classification and Rating Administration replaced the Motion Picture Code, which was a censorship operation, with a rating system. Motion picture producers/distributors voluntarily submitted their films for classification to the board, which was a creation of the motion picture companies and theater owners. The rating system was designed to give parents advance information to help them decide whether a film was appropriate for their children.

About that time, American motion pictures began to emulate foreign films in sexual explicitness and exploitative violence. Before cable offered viewers HBO, Cinemax, Showtime, where films now run unedited, editing for over-the-air broadcast generated much controversy and put me and my staff in the middle of some complicated and often contentious battles.

When we "edited for television," the production community and some critics accused us of destroying the artistic integrity of the movie. On the other side, those concerned about what children watched and advocates of traditional values questioned the arrival of controversial movies directly into the home. *Goodbye Columbus, The Last Picture Show,* and *Midnight Cowboy* are examples of the kinds of movies that stirred up these advocates.

We used the same standards to review theatrical motion pictures as we did for movies made for television, but dealing with a finished product created many more difficulties than working from a script through the final answer print. The theatrical movies gave us less room to finesse tricky situations. Some producers did provide cover shots and outtakes or had shot additional footage to substitute for material to be deleted, but ingenuity was required to implement standards without cutting up the movie, including the use of lift scenes (repositioning or repeating scenes), voice dubs, transposing, and other editing techniques.

At ABC, we established a special team to review and edit theatrical films. Robin Graham, a careful, intelligent, caring, and literate woman, would screen the theatrical feature film at first for acceptability of the overall theme and tenor. She considered questions regarding violence and sex, issues and advocacy, blood and nudity, propaganda and accuracy. If Robin found the movie could be edited to make it acceptable, she prepared a detailed script-edit report, which indicated where an edit, a deletion of a word, or elimination of a scene was required.

Her report then went to Andre de Szekely, a brilliant film editor and a former director of theater productions. He had the skill to cut a picture without making the edits obvious, and his ability to move sound around, dub words, hide nudity, cover sex scenes, eliminate blood, and quiet screams was extraordinary. More important, this Hungarian, an airman in World War II, who had been captured and escaped, had the cooperation and support of producers and directors, performers and executives who believed in him and trusted him not to ruin their work. This trust factor was as critical to his success as his editing talent. Many films would not have been broadcast on television without his cunning, suavity, and friendships.

Although they were ABC colleagues, Andre and Robin fought intense battles during the editing process; mutual respect for their often conflicting tasks was the only saving grace. When I sat in judgment as they argued their cases over whether to delete or retain a scene, I felt like a justice on the United States Supreme Court, so intense were their passions.

During the Family Viewing era,[1] ABC had a policy that required that if a movie was originally rated R, it had to be resubmitted to the Motion Picture Association of America for reclassification based upon our edits. If, in the judgment of the MPAA, our edits made the picture presentable theatrically with a higher rating than R, for example, PG, we would then accept it for telecast. The ratings were: R, under 17, requires accompanying parent or guardian; PG, parental guidance suggested, because some material might not be suitable for preteenagers; and G, general audiences.

At this time, an X rating prohibited anyone under 17 from entering the theater. This has since been changed to NC-17, which states no one 17 and under will be admitted. A PG-13 has also been added, and this urges parents to use caution, because some material may be inappropriate for preteenagers.

Although ABC continues to edit film originally produced for the large screen when they come to broadcast television, a major change took place in 1979, the time cable began to make inroads into network audiences. Changes in our practice and standards were forced by two films, *Annie Hall*, produced, written, and directed by Woody Allen, and *Looking for Mr. Goodbar*, produced, written, and directed by the late Richard Brooks.

To set the stage for our battle with Allen, the final script report for *Annie Hall*, called for the following changes or deletions:

16:30	"I was trying to do to her what Eisenhower's been doing to the country for 8 years."
22:30	"quietly humping"
23:00	"I was so close" (shots of two moving under covers in bed in dark)
32:00	"Schmuck"
32:10	"Christ"
49:25	"Mental masturbation—Don't knock masturbation, it's sex with someone I love"
50:10	"Land on your ass," "penis envy"
51:00	"We use a large vibrating egg."
56:00	"I'm sorry I took so long to finish."
56:01	"I'm starting to get some feeling back in my jaw."

Broadcast standards and practices originally requested forty-nine edits in *Annie Hall* to make it acceptable for broadcast on September 16, 1979, the opening of a new season. We were prepared to settle with Woody Allen if he agreed to make the edits of the lines listed above, but it turned out Allen and Charles Jaffe, coproducers of the comedy about sex and love, had an extraordinary contractual arrangement that gave them the right to deny the telecast of the film if Allen did not approve of the edits.

Allen refused to make any edits. His agreement was unlike those of producers of other films purchased in that he was not required to provide alternate footage or redub language or acquiesce to the Standards department's final cut. Allen had been reluctant to sell to television again, because of the edits on his *Sleeper* in the early 1970s.

We had never dealt before with certain words and situations. The use of "Jesus," "Christ," and "God" as expletives was an absolute taboo on television. Sexual references, such as "humping," "masturbation," "penis," and "crap," were always blue penciled and edited. ABC had no idea how the stations would respond if they would air the film, or how advertisers would react. We felt our list of ten was the minimum necessary to air the film, and we asked for a meeting with Allen and Jaffe.

One afternoon in July we took our list to Allen's office on Fifty-seventh Street in Manhattan, not far from the ABC headquarters. Woody Allen paced the floor as I made my most eloquent plea about how much we admired his work, which had won four Oscars, including Best Picture, and how much we wanted to show the film to a much larger audience on television, but that we had this important responsibility to act in the public interest. I explained in detail the problems in getting the stations to clear the film and our concerns about advertisers pulling out.

Allen was stoic and said, "No!"

Okay, I responded, perhaps we could just edit the jaw line, the reference to schmuck, the masturbation reference.

Again the stoic "No!"

Okay, you can have schmuck.

"No!" Polite, cordial, adamant, and a purist, Allen refused to change his mind.

Dejected and defeated, we returned to report our failure to management.

Then I began to consider what if? Perhaps? Maybe? What if we were to honor his purism? What if we left the lines in and warned the audience? As I rationalized, I began to ask if there were room for more risk taking in acceptability. Woody Allen was known and accepted for the films he made.

The era of selective or appointment viewing had begun. With millions of homes now viewing unedited films on cable or over-the-air pay television, was it time to test the waters? There was nothing graphically or visually troubling in the film. Because of the awards, viewer expectations of a Woody Allen movie, and the cinematic quality, and perhaps with an appropriate advisory, it would merit special treatment. We decided to go with the unedited version of *Annie Hall*.

I believe advisories must be used with caution to avoid making them more promotional than informational. These television warning labels must inform, but not exploit, and must never be used to attract an audience. Also, I feel strongly that advisories must not editorialize or preach.

With those precepts in mind, BS&P devised the following audio and video caution to precede the film: "The following Academy Award winning film contains explicit dialogue which may not be suitable for younger viewers. Parental discretion is advised." All promotional material and paid advertising noted "explicit dialogue" and "parental discretion advised."

After a prescreening for the affiliated stations, only one station refused to clear the movie, giving ABC 98.5 percent coverage. Advertisers were generally supportive, only three and one-half minutes of twelve commercials had to be replaced because of defections. After the telecast, 155 calls of complaint were received in New York City. Many of the complaints expressed concern that the movie had been very poorly edited and some stated that it was "chopped up."

Tom Shales, in the *Washington Post,* September 25, 1979, wrote, "'Annie Hall' will eventually be just a footnote in the history of television censorship, but at the moment it seems more than a new chapter." It was a watershed.

For us at ABC, it was a key shift. I learned that standards are not set in cement, but are guides to decision making. We operated in the subjective realm of measuring consensus, which required flexibility to respond to changing circumstances. Because the language used in *Annie Hall* was intended neither as salacious or sensational, but as realistic, intelligent dialogue in an adult film, it was a natural progression in a climate of change. Taste and style were major factors. Certainly, the quality of the work was a determining factor, but the television audience itself was growing up with the medium.

In the early 1980s, we came to another major crossroads. As I mentioned earlier, ABC for many years had resubmitted all R theatrical motion pictures with our edits for a new rating by the MPAA before its telecast, because of congressional hearings about sex and violence on television, station owners' anxiety about viewers, and the need for advertiser acceptance. This had been our procedure since the late 1960s. If a theatrical movie was rated X, we would not accept it for telecast under any conditions.

Midnight Cowboy fought and won an R rating, because, I believe, the producers were concerned in part about not being able to sell the film to television. At that time, the MPAA never published reasons for a rating, but today newspaper descriptions sometimes contain explanatory language. At ABC, we had the sense that films were given an R rating because they contained nudity, extremely graphic language or violence, the forbidden four-letter words, or a combination of these elements.

When a film was rated R, we invariably would edit it to reduce the sexual content, eliminate unacceptable language, and reduce the violence to acceptable levels. In essence, our goal was to make the film PG. After this effort, we wanted to let the viewers know that we were not telecasting an R movie. This also made it easier to get station acceptance and to sell advertisers. When necessary we would also air an advisory or disclosure statement about the film.

To keep us from falsely deciding that we had achieved our goal, we had a contractual agreement with the distributor from whom we licensed the film to resubmit the film to the MPAA for reclassification. This gave us another level of review and confirmation of our editorial process. ABC was the only network to adopt this procedure, which we used for almost ten years.

We often referred to the practice in testimony before various congressional hearings and received favorable acknowledgments for our efforts. We felt this double review showed reasonable care, public-interest awareness, and responsiveness to the concerns expressed about the effect of television on behavior.

The procedure came under fire in the late 1970s when Prof. Richard Heffner became chairman of the Classification and Rating Administration at the MPAA. He wanted to stop the practice, because he did not want to be put in the position of censor. He also said that he did not want to be involved in review for reclassification. I think he would have discontinued the practice if he had not been pressured by the major studios, who were the distributors to television and were saddled with a contractual obligation to seek a reclassification review.

Our bargaining position with the studios before the advent of cable and VCRs was strong enough to require a review as a major condition of sale to ABC-TV. Distributors agreed. I believe CBS and NBC let us carry the ball, because we established an editing standard for motion pictures before telecast, which became customary industry standard.

In 1979 and 1980, shifting economic realities forced a new direction for broadcasters. Unedited major motion pictures appeared on cable, and VCRs gave home viewers the freedom to rent or purchase unedited movies. The movie that changed our policy was *Looking for Mr. Goodbar*, produced and directed by a talented and strong-willed artist, the late Richard Brooks.

Brooks had been producer, writer, and director of such outstanding movies as *The Blackboard Jungle, Cat on a Hot Tin Roof, In Cold Blood,* among others. In *Goodbar,* he had fashioned a critically acclaimed motion picture, starring Diane Keaton and Richard Gere, that had been nominated for an Academy Award.

Looking for Mr. Goodbar was the story of an emotionally and physically handicapped young woman with a repressed religious experience, who self-destructs as she seeks to escape her past. Convinced of her unattractiveness, she indiscriminately engages in a series of graphic sexual encounters to get confirmation of herself from her lovers. A frank film, it was full of unacceptable language, including four-letter words, scatological references, vivid descriptions of sexual organs, orgasms, the taking of God's name in vain, and so forth. The portrayals of sex were candid, and the murder/rape scene, filled with graphic violence and sexuality, was the most sensational of the time.

Of the 135 minutes and 51 seconds of the theatrical version, 21 minutes and 8 seconds were excised. Two hundred forty-five deletions, totaling 115 picture edits, were made. Thirty-six times language was dubbed to change the word or expression. Sixteen picture substitutions, 71 video edits, and 130 audio deletions were made. Nineteen audio effects were generated to cover sound unacceptable, and five new special effects were created. Two minutes and five seconds of new footage was added.

Much was done with the cooperation of Richard Brooks, working with Andre de Szekely, Robin Graham, Julie Hoover, and myself. The murder scene was edited, cut, and resequenced. Dr. Mel Heller, our psychiatric consultant, reviewed the picture and made suggestions that were incorporated in the editing process. He held a seminar for editors in Los Angeles and used the film and its editing as a model teaching case. He even suggested changing the title.

Arthur Barron, a vice president of Paramount Pictures, after the telecast on May 18, 1980, and after some eighteen months in editing and review, thanked Andre de Szekely for his efforts and cooperation in the editing. "I must say it was the biggest struggle I have ever experienced in all my years in this area."

Army Archerd, in his *Daily Variety* column of Friday, May 13, 1980, "Just for Variety," quoted Brooks as saying he was "horrified" by the way his picture aired on ABC. "I thought I had the right to cut it for TV, but I found I didn't. It wasn't the same movie. Not every movie is right for TV."

The movie ran with an advisory at the opening and again before the second act. It said, "Tonight's film is a sexually frank portrayal of a young woman's self-destructive search for personal identity. Although edited for television, this film may not be suitable for younger family members. Parental discretion is advised."

The film's R rating was never reclassified by the MPAA. After an initial edit session in late November 1979, the picture was submitted in the usual manner to the MPAA for reclassification, and we were told the film still could not be classified as PG.

After that, I rescreened the movie and submitted the version to Dr. Heller. I had an unpleasant conversation with Heffner, the chairman of the Rating and Classification Administration, on December 13, as I tried to find out what more we needed to do to achieve a PG rating. I became angry and frustrated, because I received no help from him.

I believe he thought the time had come to end this practice, a practice he categorized as one in which I was putting myself in the untenable position of trying to hold the MPAA to our "ancient" pledge not to show R rated films. I threatened to call a press conference and "go public" about the dispute.

On December 26, I wrote to Dr. Heffner and advised him that we were asking Paramount Pictures to resubmit the reedited version. We had made thirteen additional edits, deleting an additional eight minutes and twenty seconds from the picture. Three scenes were substantially reedited. The death scene, an especially violent and sexually graphic rape/murder, was drastically cut. An additional forty-nine seconds, which is a long stretch by movie standards, were eliminated in the lovemaking scene between Terry (Diane Keaton) and Tony (Richard Gere), which was followed by his dance with the knife. Approximately two minutes was taken out of the lovemaking, drug-snorting scene between Tony and Terry.

I reminded Dr. Heffner that over the previous eight years, 1971–79, the MPAA granted a rerating of R to PG on fifty-eight separate occasions. These included *Shampoo, Taxi Driver, Such Good Friends, Midnight Cowboy, Summer of '42, Deliverance, X, Y and Zee* among others.

I argued that the reclassification process had been a long-standing policy of ours, all on the public record. I stated that it was our judgment and that of Dr. Heller and of management who had screened the picture with us that the reedited version contains the barest minimum of necessary lovemaking and violence scenes essential to retain the story and dramatic integrity of the movie.

The procedure, I told him, had a pro-social public-oriented effect and was of great value in carrying out our duties to air theatrical motion pictures appropriately edited for home viewing. I asked his and the MPAA board's cooperation in continuing this worthwhile effort. No sale. On December 31, Richard Heffner closed the door.

In a forthright and reasoned-position letter, Heffner set the grounds for divorce. His first concern was the distinction between the motion picture industry's film classification system and our standards and practice guidelines and procedures. He argued the MPAA did not censor and barred nothing from the screen, but only provided a range of classifications, which were communicated to the paying audience.

In Heffner's view, the broadcaster, ABC in this case, had one of two choices: to permit something to appear on television or to prohibit it. In his distinction, we were censors; the MPAA were classifiers.

In my reply, I took issue with that position. I questioned whether or not ABC was indeed more censorial when it edited than the MPAA when it labeled and classified. I contended that an X rating is a prohibition. Anyone under seventeen cannot attend. An R rating prohibits anyone under seventeen from attending without a parent or guardian. I also argued that because we edited material, we increased our options, which enabled us to present certain restricted material to a broader audience.

Heffner stated that "we embrace our opportunity at once to serve both the public interest and the motion picture industry's various private interests merely by signaling parents as to what we believe they will consider the general level of 'maturity' of an individual film's content so that they can make their own decisions about their own children's movie going."

On the other hand, I contended that our practice was no more or less than the exercise of editorial judgment, subjective as it might be, in a visual medium. We took a given project, one well-known to our audience, because of its prior theatrical release, reviewed it, sometimes discussed it with consultants, edited it, and aired it. We often wrote an advisory when warranted, which obviously *Looking for Mr. Goodbar* did.

ABC, I noted, modified both the structure and the presentation itself to exercise a degree of care, not unlike the MPAA's, as it advised parents in order to create a presentation suitable for a mass medium. We did this with many interests in mind, including the public, the network, the affiliated stations, the advertiser, and the creator.

The basis of our judgment also came into question. Does one consider what has been taken out? Does it alter what's left in? How important is critical acclaim? What of aesthetics? Heffner insisted that the board rates film "as we believe parents would have us rate them." We insisted that the final decision as to air-worthiness was ours. We tried to balance public interest as an invited guest in the home and retain the creative integrity of the film.

The board never did look at the film after it was resubmitted by Paramount, and Heffner advised that it would still be rated R.

After *Looking for Mr. Goodbar*, we no longer submitted our edited theatrical movies for reclassification. Our exchanges ended the marriage. The picture ran at 9 P.M. EST on May 18, 1980, with the advisory previously described.

A press release was prepared, which stated,

> This film was carefully reviewed and edited by the Department of Broadcast Standards and Practices, as well as our outside psychiatric consultant, Dr. Melvin Heller. Edits were made which, in our opinion, made this film appropriate for network telecast.
>
> The use of the MPAA to review films has, in many instances, become counter-productive inasmuch as we do not share either the same standards or objectives. Their evaluation of material, therefore, became increasingly inconsistent with ours.

The press release was never issued.

In one of life's ironic twists, the television ratings system put into effect in the late 1990s has as its progenitor the MPAA Classification System. The man most responsible for its adoption and promulgation is Jack Valenti, the executive to whom Dr. Heffner reported and who I have to believe knew of our debate and difference of opinion.

Movies Made for Television

The ABC movie of the week, MOW, was developed by Barry Diller, a bright, brash, young former talent agent who joined ABC programming in his climb to prominence in the communications industry. Diller had been put in charge of theatrical motion picture acquisitions, the licensing of movies originally made for theatrical distribution. Because of the importance of these movies to the networks, the costs soared. Unless the theatrical movie was a blockbuster, a James Bond or a Clint Eastwood action-adventure, the license fee for two runs often outweighed the cost-per-thousand return.

NBC pioneered the concept of movies made for television in the late 1960s, but they purchased these movies from other suppliers. Diller's idea was for ABC to produce its own movies, which would provide the network with a program needed for Tuesday night. The first movie of the week ran ninety minutes and cost approximately five to six hundred thousand dollars, a bargain for that length of a program.

In the dramatic anthology style of its predecessors, such as *Playhouse 90* and *Studio One,* and with the action and sensationalism of B movies, the first MOWs provided diverse entertainment at economically viable costs. Eventually, the format was lengthened to two hours, and the MOWs were promoted as if they were theatrical motion pictures bought for television viewing.

The new programming format, with expanded room to develop characters and plot, enticed new writers to work in television, including those who in the past had written only for theatrical movies. Diller sought provocative and controversial subjects, which opened up opportunities for writers and producers who wanted to explore previously forbidden topics. The MOWs also evolved two new forms, docudramas and miniseries, which will be discussed later.

The movie of the week became a visual library of fiction, and accelerated the end of such magazines as *Life, Look,* and *The Saturday Evening Post.* The movie format also delved into news stories of personal trials and tribulations, victories and defeats, scandals and abuses. This dramatic treatment of nonfiction, real life, blurred the lines between news and entertainment and pushed television programming into previously uncharted and sometimes treacherous political terrain.

Today, some three decades after these movies followed Truman Capote's *In Cold Blood* into novelized truth, the blurring of news and entertainment continues to generate controversy.

As discussed previously, in the 1970s, television programming pushed the boundaries in sexual content, including the November 1972, ABC broadcast of *That Certain Summer,* the first full-length television drama to deal with homosexuality. The movie won critical acclaim and helped establish the movie of the week as a hit series.

The MOWs tackled many other controversial subjects. *Little Ladies of the Night* was about prostitution, and a *A Question of Love* was about a lesbian couple's fight over child custody. *Friendly Fire* exposed the death of a U.S. soldier in Vietnam caused by fire from American troops. *An Unmarried Woman,* which dealt with the "sexually frank portrayal of the personal relationships of a contemporary woman" ran with an audio and video advisory. *The Women's Room,* based on the novel, explored feminism, another television first.

Many of these movies marked the first television exploration of sensitive and important social issues. They also pushed my job as censor in an unexpected direction. Diller, in effect, said to me, "Find a way to make it happen," referring to these forays into controversial and previously off-limit topics.

Before, Standards and Practices had stood for restraint, compromise, and the application of guidelines to make programs acceptable to most of the people most of the time, but now my staff and I were asked to reconsider the depiction of violence, the expression of love and sex, and controversial topics. As television programming moved closer to a reflection of contemporary headlines, the censor's role in program review became an even more delicate one. We no longer defended the status quo, the comfortable consensus of the past, but helped shape the message and made judgments about how much to permit of the day's realities. That the censor's role took on new dimensions created controversies within the company itself.

As described in chapter 3, *Something About Amelia* moved television programming into the shocking and forbidden topic of incest and also awakened the audience to a serious issue. The advisory highlights the drama and its importance: "The following program deals with incest and its painful consequences. It focuses on awareness, communication and treatment for affected parents and children. The family is encouraged to view together. However, due to sensitive subject matter, parental discretion is advised."

About two and one-half months before *Something About Amelia* aired, ABC presented one of the most outstanding movies of the week ever produced. Broadcast on Sunday, November, 20, 1983, *The Day After* attracted the most controversy and the most viewers of any movie in the series. The drama detailed the imagined impact of a nuclear attack on an American city and the devastating emotional and physical aftermath of that explosion.

From the early spring of 1981, when I first heard of the project, until December 7, 1983, when I defended the broadcast to the Affiliates' Board of Governors, my life was consumed by the program. At that first early-morning meeting, I was told the program would be designed to "raise the consciousness" of viewers by presenting the "despair and destruction that a nuclear encounter could wrought upon the world . . . without making a political statement."

At the oversized oval table on the fifth floor of 2020 Avenue of the Stars, ABC Entertainment Center in Century City, California, I sat with my staff, Bret White, Tom Kersey, and members of the Program Department, Brandon Stoddard, who lacked the patience for preliminaries, stayed only for a short while, Stu Samuels, and Steve White. Our task was to set the parameters to make an acceptable presentation of the drama.

At that first meeting, Stoddard said, "This was to be a happening. What could happen when a device, a bomb exploded. Nothing more, nothing less."

Samuels added, "It would not be a polemic."

Much further down the road, shortly before the program aired, Stoddard was quoted in the *New York Times*, September 3, 1983, as saying, "It has no political discussion or bent or leaning whatever. It simply says that nuclear war is horrible." And I was quoted as saying that "that very depiction could itself be interpreted as a political statement. Graphically you are showing the core of the argument of those who are for a nuclear freeze."

That, in essence, was the difficulty of the task and the reasons for the political and public fallout before the broadcast aired. ABC took many steps to mitigate concerns about content and its impact on viewers, but on that first morning, our goal was to hammer out a framework for a drama that dealt with a pressing political and social issue. BS&P wanted a drama that in word or picture did not preach. It should neither advocate the deterrence by creating a public outcry for disarmament nor support "Peace Through Strength" by espousing a military and nuclear buildup.

How were we to present a program that would deal with death, devastation, vaporizing of human beings, firestorms, burnt flesh, miles of hospital cots, misery, frustration, stillness, darkness and apathy, and loss of friends, family, countrymen without making a statement?

Here we were, two and one-half years before the telecast, planning a scenario that could very well take place in real life in that cold war world. The censors and the programmers agreed we would try to maintain a sense of objectivity in presenting this difficult and controversial subject in a socially responsible manner.

In reality, this meeting marked the beginning of a protracted battle between BS&P and the programming department, whose primary interest was to get the drama aired, regardless of the public debate. As the air date grew closer and the political controversy escalated, the programming department was delighted.

Several conflicting objectives had to be addressed. To tell the story and keep the audience interested required a certain amount of dramatic license. After all, this was fiction, a drama, not a documentary. In those years of verbal and military antagonism between the Soviet Union and the United States, the relevancy of the drama to political fears and fevers meant great care had to be taken with factual representation, scientific accuracy, and point of view.

From the BS&P perspective, it had to be done "matter of fact." We didn't want a dramatic treatment that propagandized for either side of the debate over nuclear weapons. Our affiliates, who would have to clear the program, could not be put in a position that left them vulnerable to economic and social pressure. This was equally true for the advertisers, who would pay the bills.

Two core notes were set down in that first meeting to guide development. One centered on a fair and balanced presentation of opposing points of view regarding the possible use of nuclear weapons. The view that there is a need for military preparedness and nuclear capabilities as facts of life needed further examination in any subsequent development. The stance of the project should avoid taking any position on disarmament proposals, but should pose both sides of this controversy from a straightforward and unbiased position.

The second point focused on the need to discuss depiction of the visual effects of people caught in the nuclear strike. Although BS&P acknowledged the need for realistic portrayal, we said viewer digestibility and questions of taste must be addressed.

Brandon smiled and "acquiesced." He had one of the best writers in the business, Ed Hume, prepared to write the script. Stu Samuels tried to set up negotiating points to give himself flexibility. After all, he and Steve White were the line operators responsible for the production. Bret White of my staff also looked for specifics as to what it meant to say the presentation had to reflect an accurate political military, and social scenario. BS&P would require substantiation for such elements as deployment of nuclear weapons, the strike and its aftereffects, and the medical information, some of which was speculative.

The first and second drafts accelerated the dialogue between the censors and the programmers. BS&P engaged Dr. Harold Brode as our scientific consultant, and Tom Kersey assigned Kathy Stephens, a thoughtful and controlled editor, as our first line of defense. Dr. Brode, a former senior physicist with the Rand Corporation, at the time vice president of strategic programs with the Pacific Sierra Research Corporation, had been an adviser to NATO, to the Swiss and Swedish governments on nuclear protection, and on civil defense.

Upon reading the first draft, Brode made a number of technical comments about the effect, size, and portrayal of the blast. Of greater importance to me was his first evaluation of the script, reported in a memo from Kathy Stephens to Kersey, in early March 1982. She wrote:

> In general, Mr. Brode's reaction to the script was positive. He felt that the story would serve a useful purpose in that it showed people surviving, and pulling together in learning to cope with the aftermath. He felt it was pretty well balanced, and closer to reality than the doomsayers whose dire predictions preclude any survivors whatsoever. It is true that the devastation would be unprecedented and perhaps too horrible to contemplate, but to indicate that there would be no survivors would be misleading and simply not true.
>
> On the other hand, the civil defenders who would say that everyone can survive if we all have shovels and can dig a shelter are being overly optimistic, so this script portrays a responsible middle ground. He felt that the scenario was realistic—the targets in this country are essentially military, but close lying civilian centers will be in the line of fire also.
>
> In terms of accuracy, he said he was not uncomfortable with the treatment effects—with the exception of the notes given. The depiction of the blast itself is valid—all hell breaks loose, things go to pot, there is no surviving electrical power, etc.
>
> He gave general notes on the depiction of the blast itself: the flash would be brighter than anything conceived, stronger than the sun. The

first reaction would be to turn away from it, to somehow duck. The light is so intense, it causes everything to smoke, even metal. This creates clouds of dust and fine particles. He envisioned an effect such as the screen going pure white, totally overexposed, then fading back into an image. It would be edifying to have more than one blast, as multiple blast problems would be clearer to understand.

After reading the second draft, Brode's comments were generally positive, but he had two primary concerns about fallout and residual radiation and ultraviolet damage to the ozone layer. He contended the fallout from a nuclear strike would be much worse, and he felt the script overstressed the impact on the ozone layer.

After screening the rough cut in early December 1982, Brode had a mixed reaction to the film. Striving for accuracy in simulated scenes was indeed difficult. He had little problem with the re-creation of the blast sequences, approved use of old blast footage, and gave notes for changes in the special effects of flashes, fireballs, mushroom cloud formations, smoke, and the like. He felt the handling of the radiation victims was good without being overly grim. The epilation, festering sores, loss of hair, and so forth, were all well done. He had questions relating to credibility. There needed to be more fades, and the distant fireballs and mushroom clouds were too sharply defined and dark.

His greatest concern was with the EMP, the electro magnetic pulse material, and representations. He took issue with the inference that all cars would stop and all electricity would go out. Modifications would have to be made. At least one or two cars should start up after the blast. The hospital generator would probably not be interrupted. The ozone layer would not be totally destroyed, and the atmosphere would be dark, cloudy, with lots of particles that would almost block the sunlight.

He also suggested that when Oakes, played by Jason Robards, returns to his home in Kansas City, everything would be flat and burned with no crater holes. Some of the concerns could be met by editing and changes in dialogue. We had footage added showing batteries in use and flashlights held over the operating tables. Static was added for radios, but we capitulated and gave wide latitude for reasonable dramatic license.

Because those who researched the possible effects of nuclear deterioration would be aware of the inaccuracies and overstatements, Dr. Brode requested that his name not appear in the credits, and we agreed. Although he was not thrilled with the details of accuracy, philosophically, Kathy Stephens reported that he felt the film dealt with a difficult subject that would put it on a middle ground. There would be those who would say that the film did not show the true horror and consequences of a nuclear occurrence—total destruction—and there would be those who would believe that the possibility of survival had been underplayed.

BS&P insisted and got a more ambiguous portrayal of events leading up to the bombing. Uncertainty as to who pressed the button first was not a problem. Stoddard, Robert Papazian, the producer, and Nicholas Meyer, the director, agreed with that requirement of ours, but the dramatic "reality" of an attack made it impossible to eliminate the making of a political statement.

BS&P did cut down on political discussions or polemics, but lines such as "If you were in utero and had any choice in the matter, would you be dying to be born into a world like this," and sardonic references to warnings of impending catastrophe with statements such as "but no one was interested" remained in the dialogue.

In a 1982 ABC press release, part of ABC's efforts to control the debate and diffuse the criticism, Stoddard was quoted as stating that the film would "provide an unrelenting and detailed view of three nuclear explosions in and around Kansas City, and what the effects might be on average American citizens, far removed from political origins or explanations. It is not [to be] a story of war rooms, hot lines, and cabinet meetings, but a drama about ordinary people immediately before, during and after a massive nuclear attack."

With all the concern over "political overtones," we still could not forsake questions of taste, which ranged from scenes in the hospital, viewer tolerance for the depiction of sores, lesions, loss of limbs, and nudity, to reference and dialogue about a diaphragm.

From the first script note, we asked for the elimination of all action and dialogue referring to a female character's running to her room to get a diaphragm, her younger sister running off with it, and the character's lament about using birth control. BS&P did relent about the last statement, because it was about hope for the future. In the making of a drama about a topic of such political significance, what a strange footnote to describe negotiations over the forbidden use in 1983 of the word *diaphragm*. Nuclear holocaust, but not birth control.

In the political arena, some conservative groups were concerned about balance. The Reverend Jerry Falwell, who led the conservative religious Moral Majority Organization, and Reed Irvine, the chairman of Accuracy in Media, a conservative watchdog group, were noisy in the newspapers and ominous to advertisers. Falwell threatened to urge a boycott of the sixteen companies who had bought time in *The Day After*. Reed Irvine wrote

Leonard Goldenson, ABC chairman, charging ABC was being used as a channel for Soviet propaganda. The American Legal Foundation, a non-profit conservative organization that monitors the media, threatened to sue ABC if viewers suffered serious emotional fallout.

Jake Keever, vice president of sales at ABC, previewed the film for advertisers and agencies to "alleviate advertiser concerns." He had a seven-million-dollar film to sell in a hostile environment. ABC agreed not to schedule commercials after the bomb exploded, which placed most of the twenty-five thirty-second spots in the first hour of the broadcast. Some spots went for bargain prices as low as $60,000 to $67,000 each, but the average reached $100,000, about $25,000 below the average cost of a commercial in 1983. The first network run generated only $2.5 million in advertising revenue. By the time revenues accumulated from foreign sales, ABC managed to make $9 million on the film, hardly a lucrative adventure for such maximum effort.

To meet the concerns of conservatives and to ensure a balance of views, Roone Arledge, president of ABC News, was persuaded to schedule an ABC News *Viewpoint* with Ted Koppel as host after the telecast of *The Day After*. The program featured a broad spectrum of panelists with diverse political opinions about nuclear readiness and preventive measures. It included a special interview with then secretary of state, George Shultz, and the panel consisted of former secretary of state Henry Kissinger, William F. Buckley Jr., Robert S. McNamara, former defense secretary, scientist Carl Sagan, and author Elie Wiesel.

In a previously scheduled appearance on Thursday, November 17, 1983, three days before the telecast, I appeared at a public forum on the campus of Arizona State University and stated that the intent of the picture was to decrease "the denial factor" among the public that a "nuclear holocaust" could occur and to increase viewer awareness of its implications. I also reiterated the telecast had no relationship to the deployment of Pershing II missiles in Europe. In fact, just days before I had ordered that all references, both audio and video, to Pershing missiles be deleted from the picture.

Nuclear politics, however, was only one aspect of the controversy. Many psychologists and educators warned of dire consequences for children exposed to *The Day After*. Dr. Dorothy Singer, Yale University, Family Television Research Center, was quoted in a *New York Times* article saying, "The sense of loss suffered by the families on the screen may promote profound fear about children's separation from parents. I fear children will have nightmares about the show and worry about it for weeks or even months. Older children and adults may have a sense of hopelessness."

Dr. Helen Caldecott, representing Physicians for Social Responsibility, came down from Cambridge to ask ABC to move the program to a later time than its intended start of 8 P.M. EST on Sunday evening. The National Education Association, the U.S.'s largest educational organization, issued its first ever parent advisory on a television program. The NEA recommended that parents should not, under any circumstances, allow their children to watch alone. School districts issued warning to parents and in some locations sent letters home advising parents that school-age children should not watch the movie at all.

To assess and alleviate these concerns, BS&P took a number of steps. The ABC Social Research unit undertook a review of the literature and learned that 40 percent of American children knew about nuclear weapons by the time they were twelve and some as young as six. The research also suggested that children felt a need for more information and wanted to talk about it.

Screenings were held for child psychiatrists, developmental psychologists, and child educators. Mel Heller, our in-house consultant, screened the film with me and was influential in my reversing a decision on one scene that had gotten into the film. It showed a distraught child, sitting up, screaming, and then the screen went to black. The creative people wanted to retain the scene as an exclamation point. I argued that it would be considered excessive. I lost the first round, but with Mel's support got the cut. Other consultants predicted younger children would not grasp the full impact of the movie and might even be bored. Some believed children would want to discuss what they saw with adults and would channel their reaction into an educational experience.

The ABC Social Research unit then conducted a qualitative focus group to determine children's actual reactions. Two months before the airdate the film was screened for two groups of children and their parents. Twenty-seven children were divided into two age-groups, ten to twelve and thirteen to sixteen years. Dr. Ian Alger, professor of psychiatry at the Einstein College of Medicine, served as consultant.

The findings showed no immediate adverse emotional reactions to the film were observed by either children or parents. Although most experienced sadness and fear, all were able to deal comfortably with their emotions. Young children, those ten to twelve, as expected, were bored with the first forty minutes and the last third of the motion picture, scenes that were low in action. They perked up and were very attentive during the scenes that showed the firing of missiles and the nuclear explosions.

Also, as predicted by cognitive developmental theory, the younger children did not understand the abstract global issues presented in the film. They experienced it concretely and were upset by the portrayals of death, destruction, and the separation of family members, events to which they could relate from their experiences. Older children and adolescents were able to abstract the more far-reaching implications, the actual possibility of an attack, the concept that could spark depression and hopelessness.

All of the focus group viewers, children and adults, wanted to talk about what they had seen. They also had many questions about the events portrayed in the film and the issues raised. The younger children talked mostly about the characters, but older children discussed how to prevent or cope with a nuclear attack. A common thread ran through the comments of all the viewers that *The Day After* was a must-see for everyone.

To evaluate the children's long-term emotional reactions to the movie, the parents were interviewed by telephone one to two weeks later. No nightmares, sleeplessness, or emotional disturbance of any kind were reported. Most parents said their children discussed the film with them and other family members on the day of viewing or the following day, and some talked about it with their friends. Mostly, by the time of the follow-up, *The Day After* was not an important issue for the children. The parents, however, were anxiously awaiting the day of broadcast and were caught up in the prebroadcast nationwide discussion.

To emphasize our recommendation that children who watched *The Day After* be accompanied by a parent, we had John Collum, who played the father/farmer character, speak an opening prologue.

> Hello, I'm John Collum. In this evening's ABC Theatre presentation of "The Day After," I play a father in a typical American family who experience the catastrophic events of a full-scale nuclear war.
>
> Before the movie begins, we would like to caution parents about the graphic depiction of nuclear explosions and their devastating effects. The emotional impact of these scenes may be unusually disturbing, and we are therefore recommending that very young children not be permitted to watch.
>
> In homes where young people are watching, we'd like to suggest that the family watch together so that parents can be on hand to answer questions and discuss issues raised by the movie.
>
> Immediately following "The Day After," ABC will present a special edition of "Viewpoint" that will explore some of the political, military, and psychological aspects of the nuclear age.
>
> In a moment, "The Day After."

In addition, we aired an opening advisory, which was repeated in part at the last commercial station break immediately before the detonation of the bombs, and an epilogue that was to be both audio and visual: "Although based on scientific fact, this film is fiction. Because the graphic depiction of the effects of a nuclear war may not be suitable for young viewers, parental discretion is advised."

This advisory ran before detonation of the bomb: "Because the graphic depiction of the effects of a nuclear war may not be suitable for young viewers, parental discretion is advised."

After the program, this epilogue: "The catastrophic events you have just witnessed are, in all likelihood, less severe than the destruction that would actually occur in the event of a full nuclear strike against the United States. In its presentation ABC has taken no position as to how such an event may be initiated or avoided. It is hoped that the images of this film will inspire the nations of this earth, their peoples and leaders, to find the means to avert the fateful day."

The broadcast was followed by the showing of a well-balanced list of books on the topic and the ABC "News Viewpoint" program described earlier. *The Day After* received the highest rating of any made-for-television movie—with 38 million, 550,000 households tuned in to the average minute. An estimated 100 million people saw part or all of the movie.

The first indication of viewer reaction came from telephone calls. New York and Los Angeles tallied 6,624 calls after the telecast. Positive calls outweighed negative ones three to one. Only a few calls mentioned the effect of the film on children.

The ratio of letters that followed were five to one, pro to con. Overall, in an ABC Research Department survey, viewers of *The Day After* evaluated the program favorably. Over three-quarters, 77 percent, of the viewers rated *The Day After* as good to excellent; only 6 percent rated it poorly.

Very few evaluated the film in terms of controversial issues or the appropriateness of children's viewing. Two percent thought the drama made an antinuclear statement, 1 percent pronuclear. Only 2 percent commented on the issue of children's viewing, and only one-half of 1 percent felt the film was inappropriate for children.

In my December 7, 1983, appearance before the Board of Governors of the ABC-affiliated stations, I asked a rhetorical question whether it had been worthwhile, with all the anguish, pressure, and controversy, to do *The Day After?* My answer was yes. The drama did more than show the horrific aftermath of a nuclear strike; together with the "Viewpoint" program that followed, it warned both sides not to stir up passion and divisions over an issue so vital to the survival of the planet. For television to tackle this most sensitive of political issues seemed to me, then and now, an example of the highest kind of leadership by the network and the affiliates.

On June 17, 1992, almost a decade after that momentous broadcast, Boris Yeltsin, president of Russia, addressed a joint session of the United States Congress: "Despite what we saw in the well-known American film 'The Day After,' it can be said today, tomorrow will be a day of peace, less of fear and more of hope for the happiness of our children. The world can sigh in relief. The idol of Communism . . . has collapsed."

The collapse of the Soviet Union led to an abatement in the public's fear of nuclear war. Some of the voices of special-interest groups that once sounded so loud to the television networks have also disappeared. In a later chapter I will detail some of the complex relationships and debates with these groups, including some who sought to suppress the free flow of ideas to promote their own agendas.

At this point, however, I turn to the story of how good intentions went awry during the production of a movie of the week miniseries, first entitled *Hanta Yo*, which eventually aired as *Mystic Warrior*.

Mixing entertainment with social and political enlightenment is a tricky process under the best of circumstances, and when the cauldron is stirred by conflicting agendas, the competitive nature of television, and constraints of the dramatic form, the results sometimes please no one. To this day I'm not sure the steps we took in BS&P accomplished what we hoped.

Several previous attempts had been made to set the record straight about Native American culture and the misdeeds of the white man. Stan Marguiles and David Wolper had produced a two-hour made-for-television movie, the epic story of the forced march of the Nez Percé commanded by Chief Joseph, *I Will Fight No More Forever*.

After the success of *Roots*, David Wolper came to Brandon Stoddard with Ruth Beebe Hill's book, *Hanta Yo*. The story, written by a white woman of the Northwest, with the aid of a consultant and friend, Chunksa-Yua, was about the traditional culture, lifestyles, living habits, and religious beliefs of Native Americans. Sweat lodges and vision quests, medicine men and mysticism, love and sex, and authenticity of language and custom were all depicted and described in the minutest of detail. Of greater significance was the discourse on the dignity of the human experience in relation to the earth and the environment. This story about the Oglala Sioux, the Lakota Nation in Pine Ridge, North Dakota, was also a treatise about American Indian philosophy and religion.

Because the novel was based on fact, we faced questions about accuracy. We had to consider stereotyping, point of view, and the truthfulness of the representation. Early on we found ourselves in a swirl of controversy generated by conflicts among Native Americans. Some, who believed in assimilation and wanted to discard ethnic customs, traditions, and old values, opposed the program completely. Their concern was that once again the American people would look upon their people as "savages" and the program would solidify stereotypes.

On the other hand, with great pride, others felt the American people had never understood Indian culture, Indian values, or the emphasis of Native Americans on sustaining nature and the planet. Those with this view saw the program as an opportunity to educate and right wrongs.

I was introduced to the late Louis Bad Wound, a world traveler and Native American sage, who sat and explained the culture. While he was not supportive of the book, he accepted it as a vehicle and outlined what would be required to win support from those he represented. He could not speak for everyone, but would carry our intentions to the elders, and give us their thoughts and feelings.

To answer attacks from the opposition, including Joalln Archanbault, an Indian anthropologist and academic, and literary figures such as Vine De Loria and Bea Medicine, I sought the counsel of Chief Oren Lyons of the Onandaga Nation. Introduced by my friend, the late Ann Maytag, Chief Lyons patiently explained the ways, the values, the beliefs, and the significance of the circle. I think he had doubts about my ability or willingness to absorb and accept his case, because of my business background, but I believe he felt he kindled a light of understanding.

I had dinner at an elegant east side Manhattan restaurant with Ruth Beebe Hill, who was angry and hurt over being questioned about her lifelong effort and twenty-five years of research to capture the story of the Oglala in the Lakota tongue. She was adamant that her story reflected the traditional culture and life style faithfully and provided significant anthropological and historical information for a vast untutored audience.

Louis Bad Wound and Larry Red Shirt, in all their finery, with covered peace pipe, and I had dinner with David Wolper to give him their thoughts and to emphasize the need for accuracy and authenticity and minimum amount of dramatic license. Although certainly a scholar and dedicated documentarian, Wolper, nevertheless, knew he would have to take certain liberties to create an entertaining drama.

I dined with Russell Means at the Madison Hotel in Washington, D.C., where at first the headwaiter refused to seat an American Indian who was not wearing a coat and tie. Means explained the conflicting points of view and offered his services in the production.

The production was postponed for several years as the controversy festered, but BS&P continued its research. Robin Graham of our staff prepared voluminous notes, including the description and scripted depiction of traditional ceremonies, customs, and living habits. We corroborated mystical and religious references in several different texts. We were careful in screening the sun dance to ensure the correct words, the correct time of year, and a realistic but minimal tearing of the flesh during the ceremony.

An adviser and staging consultant was engaged. George Amiotte and George American Horse were on the set during shooting to ensure accuracy of detail. Casting was reviewed with Indian representatives in Hollywood. Tempers flared, and political pressures were placed on the elders to disapprove and not cooperate in the production.

Wolper quietly continued to pursue the project, changing the name to *Mystic Warrior* to disassociate himself from the controversy, which now centered on "Hanta Yo" and Hill. He engaged Tim Giago, editor of the *Lakota Times*, who was respected in his community and attuned to some of the "outside" manipulation, to serve as an intermediary.

The program, which finally aired in May 1984, and was screened for representatives of the Oglala Sioux in Pine Ridge, received a great deal of praise. A bibliography after the program directed viewers to other information about Native Americans. Most significantly, the television viewers saw something much more complex and interesting than the traditional version of cowboys and Indians or the U.S. cavalry chasing down painted warriors. *Mystic Warrior* set the standard for all future media presentations of Native American customs and lifestyle.

A world away in time and in the magnitude of the project was *War and Remembrance*, the longest miniseries ever made for television. This thirty-hour epic provided another seminal experience for those of us in Broadcast Standards and Practices. Based on Herman Wouk's book, the television script adaptation was produced and directed by Dan Curtis; the project was three years in production.

Rabbi Marvin Hier, dean of the Simon Wiesenthal Center in Los Angeles, the repository of Holocaust research and investigatory works, captured the sentiment of this production in a letter he wrote me on March 29, 1988, after screening the Holocaust scenes.

> As historical consultants to the film who have been involved since its inception, I must tell you without reservation that "War and Remembrance" is the most profound and definitive work on the Holocaust that will ever be shown throughout the world. The portrayal is so real, authentic and unsanitized. There is such a special quality about it that gives one

the feeling that what is happening is actually happening at that very moment in time.

There have been so many valiant attempts to portray the story of the Holocaust. . . . The presentation of this material is what the thousands of victims . . . have been waiting for. Many of them have become convinced that the true story would never be told. That it would be romanticized and trivialized. "War and Remembrance" will change all that.

I think the film will be an epic. . . . I want to congratulate ABC for having the vision and the foresight to back such an outstanding project. It takes a good deal of courage to show this film. But every scene is authentic and backed by historical documentation. I know that there will be a lot of soul searching . . . to show all as it is.

Before filming began, Curtis came to the ABC headquarters in New York to state his case. He was going to show history "like it was," including the gas chambers, the nudity, the bestiality, the death camps, death, all of it. He told us this film would take courage and more, including a willingness to show such reality and to weather advertiser, station, and special-interest group resistance.

Not only were we concerned in BS&P about the death scenes and the events leading to the gas chambers, but also the brutality suffered by the lead character, Aaron Jastrow, and his cremation. Then there was the explicit implication that Natalie Henry, Jastrow's niece, would be required to perform oral sex to save her child's life. Besides language that had never been heard on television before, we were confronted with a number of firsts.

Dan Curtis was adamant about the scenes leading up to and including the horror of the gas chambers. Bret White, West Coast vice president of Standards and Practices, sent notes on February 26,1989, to prepare me for the screening.

Bret White, the son of a Kansas physician, was introduced to me by his brother, Ward White, counsel to Sen. Howard Baker, when I testified before a Senate committee. I hired Bret White, and he came to New York in June 1972. His vision, his sensitivity, and his ability to suggest viable solutions to difficult standards problems led to rapid advancement in the department. Then, one day in 1980, he came to me and said he had had enough and was taking off for the quiet and serenity of his father's cabin in Colorado.

Several years later, he returned to take up his old position. Now more mature and more secure in his decision making, he became head of the West Coast Department of Standards and Practices. Today, he is probably the most respected and accomplished professional in this difficult field.

In his notes, he wrote: "Auschwitz. Toughest sequence in the film. Nudity is fairly well handled. Back nudity, breasts, some female pubic areas. No male genitals. Dan would, of course, call this sequence, the whole point of his movie." The last sentence was underlined.

White also described other problems:

There is a sequence after the gassing when Aaron's body is put in the crematorium. We see the body begin to burn. I want to see this on a small screen for impact. However, this leads into a narrative sequence about Aaron's ashes being dumped into a river and blending into the Baltic ocean. It is the ultimate statement about the universality of the soul. I would like to keep.

Dan wasn't really interested in discussing notes until you had seen the film. He did say to me following the Auschwitz sequence that he hoped he wouldn't have to cut anything from what he obviously feels is the most powerful sequence in the film.

Several days later I watched the film. When we came to the scenes in question, some ten hours into the epic, we were emotionally prepared for, what other word is there, the Holocaust. Reason, tempered by emotion, led to the oft-quoted statement I then uttered, "This is not nudity. . .it is death." BS&P did not change a frame.

The oral sex scene was a different situation. Jane Seymour, the consummate actor, played this scene for all that it was worth and more. It was disturbing, revolting, abusive, sensual, and violent. I felt it would take viewer tolerance beyond a reasonable level of taste.

Judgments like these have no strictly rational explanation, but are born of years of watching programs and motion pictures, listening to viewers, advertisers, station owners and managers, public officials, colleagues, and family. My experience and background, including religious training, literature classes given by the eloquent Bobo Rudd at Hamilton College, and lectures on constitutional law given by Prof. Mark Dewolf Howe at the Harvard Law School, all go into the mix.

BS&P asked for and negotiated a small cut and a substituted long shot for one of the questionable scenes. Brandon Stoddard and Dan Curtis had persuasive abilities as experienced producers, which also influenced the decisions and the shape of the final broadcast.

One letter from a woman associated with an ABC news bureau warrants a footnote. The writer of the letter questioned why the camera showed only women with complete frontal nudity with adult males pictured from the waist up. She described this difference as biased and sexist.

I wrote back and agreed. We were more concerned with the showing of male genitalia, and that wasn't right. There were scenes with male genitalia, but less obvious, somewhat quicker cuts, as men cramped and huddled and shuffled in and through the gas chambers.

A few anecdotes about the BS&P edits of such a massive work don't do justice to the intensity of the process, which will probably never be repeated. Such an expensive project, $130 million, is unlikely to be undertaken again, nor is it possible to conceive of engaging an audience for such an extended period. A few four-hour miniseries are under consideration, but the era of the multinight blockbuster is over.

Many of the made-for-television movies were based on real-life events and people, which will be discussed in greater detail in the chapter on the docudrama. Occasionally, a highly controversial issue would be given a fictional treatment, which would engage BS&P in a difficult dialogue with the producer/writer. Our concern for balance and fairness about an issue of intense public conflict clashed with the creative prerogatives of the dramatists.

I chose David Rintels's *The Execution of Raymond Graham,* because it illustrates the conflict between the positions of censor and author. This was to be an especially difficult debate for me. I respected David not only as a gifted and accomplished writer, but considered him a friend with depth of vision, intellect and humanism. David Rintels's view, as I understood it, was that if an author's facts are accurate, he should have the unfettered right to present his point of view without the burden of presenting the other side. To deny the writer the freedom to advocate responsibly was to deny him exercise of First Amendment freedom of speech.

My argument, as censor in that and many, many other such internal debates, was that to serve the public interest, a television drama about a controversial political issue could not present only one side of the debate. Unlike theatrical movies, dramas, or books, where many voices compete for attention and viewers are offered many choices, television's unique and powerful reach into the nation's living rooms meant a different set of rules.

The film dealt with a convict awaiting execution who seeks the governor's intervention to overrule the death penalty. Capital punishment was and is an intense public debate. Rintels made the case against the death penalty as cruel and unusual punishment. BS&P insisted on presentation of both sides to let the viewer decide—what I have always described as exposition, not advocacy.

Here are the issues we raised about the first script. Was the death penalty properly invoked? The statute in the hypothetical state called for extenuating circumstances. Were they presented forcefully enough? We asked the murder be shown as premeditated and cold-blooded, not spur of the moment as the script indicated. We also asked that the reaction of the victim's family be strengthened and their point of view expressed to balance, what appeared to us, a sympathetic portrayal of the killer. BS&P also questioned the length of time it took for the inmate to die after the lethal gas was released. Did this depiction of suffering make too strong a statement?

Rintels resented our intrusion into his creative domain and our footprints on his script's argument against the death penalty. We did infringe upon his freedom of expression for the reasons already discussed. Both sides gave a little, but neither was totally satisfied. That middle ground where conflicts are resolved often leaves this type of dissatisfaction, because censorship is an art, sometimes a messy one, and not a science.

This genre of programs—controversial, pushing the envelope, destroying taboos, enlightening, exciting, and costly—have almost disappeared from television; like the long-lost Westerns, their time may have past. Yet, in their day, these movies brought viewers an unforgettable and thought-provoking experience, and I believe enhanced the social and political dialogue on a number of important national concerns. In my view, even, or especially, the most controversial ones were worth the effort, the battles, and the cost.

Programs Designed for Children

Although it can be said that all programs are for children, whether suitable or informative or not, because of the accessibility of the medium, its ease of use, latchkey children, lack of parental supervision, and global reach, there is a special responsibility to create programs especially designed for children. The challenge is how to use the medium to educate and enlighten the children's audience and still entertain. Age has little to do with this fact; programming has to attract and hold the audience to be financially feasible.

In television's infancy, local stations created audience participation shows, where delighted and amazed children smiled or performed for the camera. Some of these locally produced shows survived for many decades, but most disappeared quickly as the medium became more sophisticated. It was also less expensive and less trouble for the stations to buy programming than produce it.

One of the pioneers in television programming for children appeared on one of the earliest network series aimed at that special audience, NBC's afternoon series *Howdy Doody*, first telecast in 1948. Bob Keeshan played Clarabell the clown on that show. In the fall of 1955, he debuted as *Captain Kangaroo* weekdays at 8 A.M. on CBS. He had joined forces with John Miller to create that program, which contained informational and enrichment entertainment for young children. In 1955, Louis G. Cowan, creator of *The $64,000 Question*, who was in charge of early-morning program development for CBS, saw the need for such a program and encouraged affiliate acceptance.

Keeshan remained at CBS for twenty-nine years, but eventually the gentle captain ran into the shoals of a different competitive atmosphere. The longest-running program with a similar feel to that of the captain, *Mr.*

Rodgers' Neighborhood, lives on PBS where different economic realities apply.

Some seven years after the captain's appearance, ABC created an afternoon weekday series, *Discovery,* which also focused on young children. Produced by Jules Power, director of children's programming at ABC, the series was one of the first to recognize a broadcaster's responsibility to provide programs directed toward children between the ages of two and twelve. The program did not last long in the weekday afternoon slot at 4:30, where it began in the fall of 1962. The next year *Discovery* moved to Sunday morning and remained on the air until 1971. It was one of the more intelligent early efforts at dealing with children's perception of the world around them.

The education of young children about sex was hardly a topic of conversation much less of television programs in those years, but, in 1965, on this award-winning series, Jules Power, produced a first, a program and a book based on one of the programs, entitled "How Life Begins."[1] Respecting the intelligence of young readers and preteens, the book, based on the television program, covered life's beginning, both animal and human, from conception to the moment of birth, an astonishing accomplishment for the 1960s.

The amount of program designed for children was hardly lavish, but the critics primarily focused on the behavioral consequences of viewing dramatic and comedic televised violence. In the mid 1970s, the question was: did Johnny punch out his sister because he saw Starsky and Hutch beat up their enemy with fisticuffs? Did the Roadrunner teach Molly to try to bounce the baby off of the floor?

As discussed in the chapter on violence, some twenty-five years later the questions remain; only the program names and characters have changed.

The second major concern, and sometimes the primary one of critics, was the influence on children of sexual content on television. How much does a child comprehend the display of sexual depictions? Are teenagers more promiscuous because they see "it" on television?

Important ancillary issues abounded. How harmful or helpful is advertising directed toward children? Which programs are designed for children? Which should be disclaimed or parents be warned about?

Today as then, many of America's favorite clichés—"children are our most valuable asset"—flew around during debates about television programming for children. The difference then was an effort ABC undertook to answer the concerns and to act responsibly toward the children's audience. Saturday morning, weekday, and special programming, designed primarily for children and teenagers, became the center of attention in the mid-1970s. The term "pro-social" was coined to set a standard for program content.

Pro-social content and quality programs, of course, had to be achieved within the framework of a commercial broadcasting company. Peggy Charren, founder of Action for Children's Television (ACT), was one of the most determined critics who helped push broadcasters and advertisers into action.

Other forces included academic researchers such as William Schramm, who wrote about the effect of television on children. Congressional critics, including Senators Dodd and Pastore, added their voices and sometimes the additional pressure of hearings. The PTA exercised its national clout as the baby boomers of the 1950s raised their own families and questioned the role of television.

The responsibility of the media, these critics said, was not only to insure that children were not harmed, but also to make opportunities available to develop skills and values conducive to positive mental growth. Pro-social material should be broadcast that would aid children to cope in a complex society. Broadcasters were urged to deal with sex roles, role modeling, ethnicity, and stereotyping. Broadcasters also were pressured to deal with a child's "inalienable right" to be intelligently and fairly informed and yet entertained.

All this "goodness" and conscience had to be placed within the framework of an advertiser-supported programming and the constitutional principles of a democratic society. Programs would have to attract an audience and keep their attention or lose a sound base of financial support. Station clearance depended upon audience acceptance and sales. The production community wasn't interested in any dictates for educational material—if it eroded the entertainment factor and lost viewers.

One thing remains the same: ratings. Sales, profits, and creative freedom are the pragmatic realities of our system, and ultimately viewers, moviegoers, and Internet subscribers, young or old, vote with their attention, that is, their dollars.

In the mid-1970s, it was true, however, that children's programming needed improvement and innovation. Three areas of programming were affected: Saturday morning cartoons directed toward children, weekday afternoon programming, and Sunday from 7 to 8 P.M. EST.

How would we at ABC respond? James Duffy, then president of the ABC Television Network, had the idea to convene the ABC Workshop for Children's Television. This workshop brought together educators, child psychologists, parents, broadcasters, producers, performers, and critics to share ideas about what television should be for young viewers.

Parents and presenters spoke for two days. Advertising agency representatives and advertisers attended. A conscience-raising and awareness umbrella opened up over the problem of how to program to children.

Out of this workshop, ABC management, programming, and standards and practices people hammered out a philosophy to guide us in a new direction. Programs must be entertaining, because children will not be bored, and boring programs would not sell.

The schedule must also include substance, whether that substance was factual information or dialogue and content that support the development of pro-social values. Children should learn how to recognize and distinguish between right and wrong. Children should discover new worlds of science, history, and language. Above all, children should have pride in themselves, in their families, and in their country.

One of the areas of most concern was that familiar territory of children: the Saturday morning cartoons. Not until the late 1960s were animated cartoons created primarily for television. Earlier cartoons were originally made for theatrical distribution and catered to both adult and child audiences. Filled with violent action, stereotypes, white and male oriented, these cartoons were the subjects of critical disdain, and research papers denounced their behavioral harm on young minds. The controversy emerged between those who argued violence is violence in whatever form, and those who exempted comedic violence from the potentially harmful category.

With the aid of Dr. Heller, our often-mentioned consultant, detailed directions and guidelines were set forth. The program department consulted with Eda LeShan, educator and author. Both the programming departments and Standards and Practices consulted with the Bank Street College of Education in New York City. Bank Street College, a graduate school of education, specializes in child development and early-childhood education. The college takes a humanistic approach to education, in which children and adults interact as a community of learners. Bank Street identified specific concerns, which centered on three key points: sex roles, role models, and age appropriateness.

Sex roles and role modeling came into play when Michael Eisner, then head of children's Saturday morning programming, saw the opportunity to create a high-action superhero cartoon series to compete with the Superman and Batman cartoons. Eisner's idea was a cartoon adventure series to be called *Superfriends*. BS&P began to mediate the dialogue between the educators and critics and programming.

Bank Street had urged us to look for balance in portraying sex roles, male and female, that would be ego strengthening and create positive self-images. Girls should not be relegated to passive traditional family and child-related roles. BS&P asked Eisner for and got a woman superhero. Boys should not feel inadequate or uncomfortably different if they did not fit the traditional male role prescriptions.

An important aspect of an appropriate role model has to do with gender, but other areas are equally critical. Bank Street said that "there is an implicit, but strong negative message to children who never see or too infrequently see their own kind (color, sex, ethnic background) in roles which they can regard as positive, favorable and capable of leadership. These comments led to the births of three new minority "Superfriends."

Eisner, who became Chairman of Walt Disney Co., which owns ABC, saw the potential to entertain and to help change the landscape for children's cartoons. A major effort was made to address which program material should be included and which excluded in terms of the children's audience.

Dr. William Hooks of the Bank Street College of Education provided a list of qualities to strive for in programs. All were keyed to the word "respect"—respect for differences, for moral values, for feelings and sensitivities of others, for oneself.

Dr. Heller outlined the guidelines for us. Programs for child viewing or programs featuring child characters require special consideration as to the following untoward factors. Don't risk antisocial modeling and imitation. Be aware of the temptation to emulate dangerous acts or stunts, confusing or frightening materials. Prejudices are acquired or learned. Television may reveal biases or prejudices, label them, expose them, condemn them. When the bully rises put him down. The racial slur is condemned. All Indians are not bad, all cowboys are not good. Avoid the depiction of children engaged in harmful or destructive acts against other children, animals, or adults. No harm to people!

Tom Kersey, a former World War II fighter pilot, a sometime writer, a stern and stoic leader of the West Coast office of Standards and Practices, was the best first lieutenant any department head could have. I asked him to make a list of "No's," of material not permitted in children's programs.

It still seems to me the best standard. The Tom Kersey List of No's:

• No uses of kidnapping/drugs/cigarettes/liquor themes
• No mistreatment of animals
• No child jeopardy
• No bondage
• No replicable devices constructed to inflict violence

- No jealousy to be rewarded
- No revenge motives
- No anti-social behaviors without consequences
- No infusion of sex, normal or erotic
- No stereotyping of minorities
- No glorification of delinquency
- No disdain, mistrust of parents
- No coercion ("do this, or else")

In the spring of 1975, amid the furor of the Family Viewing Hour debate, I met Susan Futterman, a young woman with strong convictions about the content of children's programming. Susan held a B.S. in early childhood from Mills College of Education in New York; she taught "Head Start" programs in Harlem and Newark. In addition, she had worked with Anna Freud in London in child psychoanalysis and received an M.A. in education from Harvard. She also had served as a researcher at the Center for Research in Children's Television.

Susan Futterman lectured me on what was wrong with Saturday morning programs designed for children. I hired her as manager of children's programming in the Standards and Practices department. In 1981, she wrote a position paper entitled "Children's Programming," which recognized certain basic principles and proscribed certain types of content.

Conflict is the basis of all storytelling. Children love action-adventure. No weapons of a real nature (fantasy laser guns are okay) or explosives are allowed. Minorities are included in every possible opportunity in positive roles. Great care is to be exercised with regard to imitable acts that could result in harm to a child.

Comedy was combined with adventure and emerged as a new form especially designed for children. The action came from the chase and the confrontation. Ever present humor mediated the permissible violence in the story for the child. Scooby Doo could back into his pal Shaggy, who has just had a knight's helmet fall on his head and both jump and run in separate directions.

The face of Saturday morning cartoons changed. The laughter and enjoyment were the same. Learning and awareness of prejudice, bias, and role modeling increased, but programming cartoons with pro-social aspects was not the only change in direction.

Early in 1972, the late David McCall, head of McCaffrey McCall Advertising Agency, came up with a series of three-minute animated films teaching the multiplication tables,[2] called "Multiplication Rock." This initiated "Schoolhouse Rock," a short series of animated musicals that ran within the regular cartoon series. "Multiplication Rock" was developed in consultation with Bank Street College of Education. "Grammar Rock," developed with Dr. Henry P. Beechold of Trenton State College, taught proper use of parts of speech, and "America Rock," a series on history and government developed in consultation with Prof. John A. Garraty of Columbia University, illustrated such topics as how a bill goes through Congress. Public-service messages were devised on nutrition, social behavior, and good habits.

At noon on Saturdays the schedule included a "live action" drama for older children. The *ABC Weekend Specials* were one-half or one hour programs presenting short stories from literature. They were the first "novels for television" based on books and were designed to stimulate a child's appetite for reading.

To meet the criticism about portrayals of minorities on television, BS&P sought and got a change in the "wrap-around," the introductory bridges to programs on Saturday morning. The "All Star Saturday Kids" were created by Squire Rushnell, the head of children's programming in 1977. The "kids" consisted of a black, an Asian, a Chicano, and a Caucasian, who introduced the upcoming program. In addition, an authority figure, a black mayor, was introduced into the *Dynomitt* series, and a black woman leader added to Captain Caveman and the Teen Angels. In "Bigfoot and Wildboy," a Mexican-American girl became a regular character. BS&P argued for hours to get the skin of the Supertwins in *Superfriends* changed from pink to beige and for the additions of American Indian, Japanese, and Latin woman characters, who were to be portrayed as bright, independent, and decision makers in heroic efforts.

A quiet revolution in recognizing social differences, learning opportunities, and civil rights took place in children's programs. It was a productive time, creatively, intellectually, financially. Efforts for improvement were not limited to programming. Advertisers found new guidelines dictated to them to govern the content of commercials placed in Saturday morning programs.

The National Association of Broadcasting Television Code Review Board, of which I eventually became the senior member, and its subcommittee on children's advertising had for a number of years formulated guidelines applicable to commercials directed toward children. Responding to persuasive arguments made by such advocates as Peggy Charren, Dr.s Dorothy and Jerome Singer, codirectors of the Family Television Research and Consultation Center at Yale, and Prof. Gerald Lesser of Harvard, the code promulgated such rules as:

• Children may not be directed to purchase or ask a parent to buy a product or service for them;

- Exhortative language is prohibited;
- children's program personality (host) or cartoon character may not be utilized to deliver commercial messages within or adjacent to programs in which they appear;
- Nor may real-life authority figures/celebrities deliver a personal testimonial or endorsement for a product;
- Commercials must be clearly separated from program material;
- No person who is recognized as being identified with an advertised product's counterpart in real-life, may be used as a spokesperson or endorser;
- Each commercial for a breakfast-type product must include an audio reference and a video depiction of the role of the product within the framework of a balanced regimen;
- Commercials for products such as snacks, candies, gum and soft drinks may not suggest or recommend indiscriminate and/or immoderate use of the product;
- When premiums are utilized they are subject to stringent limitations concerning allowable time, manner or visual presentation, number of items advertised, and content.

Limits were placed on the number of commercials and the time devoted to commercials in children's programs.

If special, enriched foods were to be advertised as a substitute for a meal, their purpose and nutritional value had to be featured in the advertising and supported by adequate documentation. Advertisements could not include dramatizations of any product in a realistic war atmosphere. Comparatives and superlatives were not permitted, and we did not accept commercials for vitamins or over-the-counter medications in programs designed primarily for children.

Those prohibitions and others introduced in the 1970s changed the production of advertising directed toward children and set standards for the next twenty years. One of the major battles occurred over the balanced breakfast requirement. The great debate at the time related to the nutritional aspect of sugared cereals. The critics wanted to ban advertisement of cereals in children's programming. The manufacturers provided research and nutritional expertise as to their food value. The broadcasters who were in the middle obviously had to resist unreasonable interference with the critical economic support structure, which allowed programming changes and experimentation to happen.

The advertiser resisted the weakening of the message by having to include milk, bread, juice, and reference to a balanced breakfast. The child advocates resisted the continued advertisement of sugared products. A voluntary code board drove home the guidelines on a reluctant broadcasters' constituency, which neither wanted to offend the advertiser nor deal with the wrath of special-interest groups.

The Code Authority collapsed in the early 1980s because of antitrust considerations with respect to limitations on commercial time standards and the number of announcements that could make up a commercial pod. The federal district court decision on the Family Viewing Hour case, which will be discussed in a future chapter, also sealed the fate of the NAB Code Review board. This left the broadcasting industry without a working mechanism to deal voluntarily with both program and commercial issues.

Back on the programming front, in 1972, ABC began an afternoon series of one-hour specials that dealt dramatically with the quality of life for young teenagers. *The ABC Afterschool Specials* had one common denominator: to display respect for the needs, intelligence, and sensitivity of children. Many of the programs suggested possible solutions to difficult problems encountered by youngsters.

Among the outstanding shows were: "Rookie of the Year," the story of a girl who wanted the right to play Little League baseball; "Blind Sunday," which helped young viewers understand the handicap of blindness; "Francesca Baby," about a young girl whose mother is an alcoholic; and "My Mom's Having a Baby."

Because "My Mom's Having a Baby" showed a baby being born, several special-interest groups asked for an advisory warning to state the program might not be appropriate for children. I could understand the controversy about children not being able to distinguish between reality and fantasy, but I had difficulty understanding some viewers' unwillingness to have children view, in an unsensational manner, how life begins.

Although I have never denied the responsibilities of broadcasters, I also have insisted that these responsibilities must be shared. The broadcaster's role was to continue to strive to improve the quality and diversity of children's television, but if television was to be a constructive influence in the home, parents must know what their children watch and make judgments about the suitability of specific programs for their children. Parents should also watch television with their children and use the shared viewing as a basis for discussion.

Whether a child watches five or twenty-five hours of television each week, that viewing is an important part of his life. That reality puts an awesome responsibility on the television industry and also on the adult in the household, the person who should control the television set. For parents or caregivers who pay little or no attention to children's television viewing, television is no more than an electronic babysitter, an informative and entertaining gadget whose value will vary from child to child in unpredictable, and sometimes undesirable, fashion.

On the other hand, for parents who grasp firmly their share of the responsibility, who actively involve themselves in their children's viewing experience, television can be—and will be—a significant and constructive contributor to the growth of the generation of young people that will take over where we, their parents, leave off.

After some deliberation on the request for an appropriate advisory for "My Mom's Having a Baby," BS&P devised the following disclaimer: "My Mom's Having a Baby"—a story about the beginning of life, in which you and your family can share a youngster's learning experience through actual birth."

Saturday children's programming was not an exceptionally lucrative corner of the viewing schedule, but Sunday night was. Something interesting happened in that valuable territory as a result of an FCC ruling. In the early 1970s, the Federal Communications Commission issued the Prime Time Access Rules, which were designed to curtail network dominance over programming in prime time. The intent was to encourage local stations to provide more programs of public interest in their communities. The aim was diversification, the result quite different, but that is another story.

The exception to the FCC rules for networks was permitted on Sunday evenings from seven to eight or any other hour during prime time if the networks provided programs primarily for children ages two to twelve. The FCC also stated,

> It is our expectation that networks and licensees will not abuse this exception to the rule, particularly in access-period use of network or off-network programs which, while having some appeal to children, were or are not primarily designed for them but for viewing by adults, or adults and children, and for presentation of normal commercial advertising addressed to adults.

To track the programs in this time period from 1972 to 1992 is a lesson in balancing social policy and operating profitable in an advertiser-supported broadcasting system. ABC and NBC used the children's exemption. CBS made use of another exemption for documentary and news programs to schedule *60 Minutes.*

The challenge for ABC was to present a program that would fit the definition and appeal to a broad audience, because children were not consumers of advertising products that could survive in that prime-time location. An hour of prime-time program ranged from approximately $500,000 in 1972 to $1.2 million in 1992. Networks not only had to straddle the age appropriateness requirement, but also present material that teenagers and adults would watch with their children.

Programming for that "family audience" became a lesson in innovation. It was the joint responsibility of the program department and the Standards and Practices department. The former was the developer, the creator; the latter, the reviewer and certifier that the program met the rules. The program department, tethered by subjective interpretations and much ambiguity, did not have an easy task.

Although there was no precise definition of "programs primarily designed for children ages two to twelve" for that time period, we had several guides to rely on. From the FCC Second Report and Order Docket #19622, January 17, 1975:

> The definition of children's programming is "programs primarily designed for children aged 2 through 12." The programming permitted by the exemption is intended to be only that primary designed for pre-school and elementary school children, ages 2 to 12, taking into account their immaturity and special needs. Also, while the exemption is not limited to educational or informational material, an important purpose of it is to promote the presentation of such material.[3]

Another guideline from the court decision in the NAITPD case:

> A "children"s program' is a program "primarily designed for children aged 2 through 12." A precise definition is probably unattainable, and, indeed, undesirable. No one can set boundaries to the fantasy of a child's world. Adults brave enough to enter that domain must leave behind their sense of self-assurance. A conclave of all the advertising agencies and all the station managers could not speak with certitude for the children's world.
>
> The exemption for network children's programs does not, by its own terms, exclude fiction or drama, fairy tales or poetry, nor does it prescribe what is educational or informational. It does not provide that if the rest of the family happens to be entertained, as well, the program is no longer "primarily designed for children." Of course, other factors, such as preponderance of shaving cream advertisements, might raise some doubt on that score. While the description of the category may be attacked as too vague, a more sharply defined category probably would be attacked as an intrusion by the Commission upon program content.[4]

BS&P saw the critical question as to whether a child in that age category would understand the content of the program. Certainly, we paid more attention to the older end of the category than the younger in our programming decisions. Every conceivable genre was attempted to try to capture the audience, from adapting such classics as *Swiss Family Robinson* to injecting informational and educational sermons in an action-adventure program such as *Code 3*.

The late Irwin Allen, producer of successful films such as *Voyage to the Bottom of the Sea* and *The Poseidon Adventure* attempted to meet the challenge. Irwin would write his script about firefighters and jeopardy, adventure and action, then pick up the phone and spend hours with Susan Futterman, working out scenes to make the program comply. Animals and young children were introduced. Fire safety tips were included. In the eyes of the program department, we were interrupting the dramatic flow.

BS&P was pressured to make the successful fantasy adventure program *The Six Million Dollar Man*, acceptable for the time period. Didn't the slow motion mitigate the violence? Wasn't there the lesson of good vs. evil? Weren't there lessons in science and examples of good role models? We consulted with Dr. Heller and others and finally had to say no. The program was action-adventure with no special concerns for the younger children nor could we point to any specific educational material that would benefit the higher age-group. *The Six Million Dollar Man* was scheduled at 8 P.M.

The ABC program department reached out for another classic. The *Hardy Boys* and *Nancy Drew* series of adventure books had been best-sellers and could be defended for younger groups who looked up to "big brother and sister" stories. Reading would be encouraged by references to the series of books and other stories upon which the television characters were based. In fact, book sales did increase, but not accompanied by enough of an audience for long enough to sustain the program.

In the second report and order issued in 1975 by the FCC, in Docket #19622, the commission observed in a footnote that "it appears that only NBC's Disney program would come within this exception." The Disney name gave credible guidance. Disney was commandeered. This allowed for a little broader reach. Some hours were marginally acceptable, but others fit well, and there were no complaints.

The above efforts are of interest only for the historical record in the light of two subsequent and significant deregulatory actions. The prime-time access rule was dropped in the late 1990s. New children's programming regulations were promulgated along with certain "core" guidelines for children's educational programs, which I will review later.

Although subjective judgment often gave rise to questioning whether a program or series qualified under the rule, another factor also influenced our judgment. Although Prof. Neil Postman of New York University decried the loss of the early-childhood experience, in our opinion, early childhood naïveté was being displaced by early maturity. This increased maturity and sophistication might not include all phases of childhood and adolescence, nor was this development all good, but it was a fact of life. We had to recognize that preteens had a growing awareness of their sexuality, but had little sex education.

Young viewers had an appreciation for such global issues as the environment and explorations of earth and space, but few programs for them that discussed these topics. Of course, they were exposed to real violence, in news, in war coverage, and in civil disturbances on television.

Although some critics and parents worried about this maturation and its effects, we saw a need and opportunity to deal with teenage issues. Television was blamed for the deterioration of academic success and other ills as the society underwent major changes, but the industry and its impact was only one factor. In the middle of diversification and the fast-moving Internet, many of the same questions reappear, and as urgently as in the years when the impact of television on society dominated the social and political debates.

For example, in fulfilling the requirements of the 7 to 8 P.M. Sunday period in its fourth season in the fall of 1992, ABC scheduled an episode of *Life Goes On* during which Corky (Chris Burke), a Down's syndrome–handicapped person, would marry his similarly afflicted sweetheart. Also, Becca (Kellie Martin) was in love with HIV-positive Jesse (Chad Lowe), but "recognized that her relationship with Jesse would never be consummated and would start seeing other people." Heavy stuff for twelve-year-olds, let alone the six-to-eight group. Were children growing up that fast? The whole battle of sex education, condom supply, and AIDS intelligence had brought a new condition to programs designed primarily for children.

Perhaps we sometimes gave too little credit to young viewers "growing up" as we learned when we screened *The Day After* for a group of young people eight to twelve. Contrary to the fears of their elders, they were not unreasonably frightened, but spoke of the magnitude of nuclear war and the need to avoid one. The younger children didn't understand and were often bored by the drama, but the older ones raised questions and discussed the program with their parents.

During these decades, conscious efforts were made to meet the intelligent and valid criticism of programs for children. I believe it was an enlightened era in which broadcasters sought to expand the horizon of young people and explore their receptivity to different types of issues.

In the late 1980s and early 1990s, competition increased from such new sources of children's programming as Nickelodeon, the Fox Children's Network and the Disney channel on cable. With deregulation on the political agenda, economic factors took precedence over policy. For example, broadcast networks were allowed to increase the amount of time sold for commercials. Entertainment was emphasized in program offerings instead of pro-social content, which led, in a word, to erosion.

So the cycle turned again. Children advocates began to raise their voices. The political climate changed. In the 1990s, Congress passed the Children's Television Act, an attempt to rev up the motor and meet the educational and informational needs of children.

The act limited the amount of advertising a station could carry in television programs intended for children. It also directed the FCC to consider in its review of television station license renewal application the extent to which the station served the educational and informational needs of children. In a rule-making proceeding held in 1991, the FCC held that the act did not impose any quantitative standards and that no minimum program requirement was to be imposed. The commission also decided each licensee could determine for itself with reasonable discretion how they assess the educational and informational needs of children in their communities. Much remained the same until the arrival of a new president. In 1993, the FCC put stations on notice that cartoons such as *The Jetsons* and *The Flintstones* would no longer count as "educational and informational" programming.

On July 29, 1996, President Clinton called a meeting of broadcasters, and after much cajoling got them to agree to schedule three hours of programs that were designed to meet "core" educational needs of children. In August of that year, the FCC formerly established, effective September 1, 1997, a three-hour program standard of "core" children's educational programming. It also defined such programming as programming that furthers the educational needs of children sixteen and younger in any respect, including a child's intellectual/cognitive or social/emotional needs.

This action brought some change to the mix; however, the effect of rapid technological changes, the growth of cable, the introduction of video games, and the interfacing of the internet with television has made it more difficult to legislate quality programs for children.

Rules, however well intentioned, in the arena of children's programming work only as well as the commitment of the producers and distributors. No one has set forth a Magna Carta for children's programs nor can there ever be one. One can set standards for enrichment, of values, of goodness, of learning societal benefits and seek to include them in a format, but no rules can describe the kind of storytelling that makes children dream and grow and see themselves and their possibilities expand.

Somewhere in this mix of government, social, and technological pressures, room must be made for quality programs for children. Creating and scheduling programs that children will watch, that stations will clear, and that advertisers will support in a competitive environment is the challenge broadcasters face in the 21st century. Even if the facts have changed drastically since the first efforts with which I was involved, the need for programs created for and about children remains.

Special Interest Advocacy

The first special-interest advocate I encountered was an individual, not a group, and a most influential individual: Isabelle Goldenson, the wife of the president of the American Broadcasting Company.

Jerry Lewis had been hired to produce and perform in a comedy variety show on Saturday nights in the fall of 1963. In each of the first several shows, an effort that quickly became unsuccessful, Lewis would address himself directly to the president of ABC, with remarks to "Lennie." Some were funny, some querulous, but always, in the eyes of Isabelle and other ABC executives, embarrassing and demeaning to the president of a struggling network.

Lewis had known Leonard Goldenson from Paramount Theatre days. Bob Weitman, a close associate of Goldenson's and former manager of the New York Paramount Theatre, gave Lewis and Dean Martin their start on the stage. Jerry attempted to play his relationship with Goldenson for jokes, but the audience didn't know who "Lennie" was and few laughed.

On Yom Kippur eve, a Saturday night in October, I was told by Oliver Treyz, the president of the ABC television network, to go to the Chicago studio's control room, which handled the distribution of the live signal to the East and West Coasts. With a switch on the control board, I could obliterate any further "Lennie" references Lewis might utter. I believe we missed one and got one, but it was the last time Lewis did a "Lennie" joke.

No other encounter with a special interest would be as straightforward and easily solved as the night I "censored" Jerry Lewis. Today, after many decades of social activism across the political spectrum, special interest is an umbrella term that encompasses most Americans, by one label or another, from cradle to grave.

Pressure on the media and government for attention, money, retribution, reparations, and restitution is open and familiar today, but the critical questions remain: how much pressure is too much pressure? Which tactics threaten the public good? How is creative and political freedom preserved?

Our history is complicated in this volatile arena. One of the more invidious tactics was "blacklisting." In the early 1950s, an operator of a small chain of supermarkets in Syracuse, New York, placed signs next to certain products to warn customers that purchasing these goods advanced the spread of communism. He made trips to New York City and visited advertisers and their agencies to "advise" them about whom to hire or not to hire in the programming they sponsored.[1]

Another group in New York, the American Business Consultants, which consisted of three former FBI agents, issued a newsletter entitled *Counterattack* and offered a series of monographs. On June 22, 1950, it published *Red Channels: The Report of Communist Influence in Radio and Television*, which contained two-hundred pages of detailed background information on 151 broadcast personalities who it suggested were at least sympathetic to Communist thinking. It avoided outright accusations but by innuendo and "guilt by association" sent the message of the "undesirable."

Advertisers, agencies, and networks soon set up a system of security checks to assure that anyone who was hired was not "tainted." In some instances loyalty oaths were required for new hires. Aware Inc. was formed by several conservative members of the American Federation of Television and Radio Artists (AFTRA) and individuals with American Legion and advertiser connections. Aware "cleared" performers until 1955.[2] The system was broken when John Henry Faulk won a libel case against Aware Inc. in 1962.

Also that year, an overt attempt by an advertiser to influence news reporting pushed the network to a dangerous edge. In mid-November 1962, Jim Hagerty, former press secretary to President Dwight D. Eisenhower and recently appointed vice president in charge of ABC News and Public Affairs, and I flew to Los Angeles. Our mission was to get Patrick J. Frawley, chairman of Eversharp, Inc., the parent company of the Schick Safety Razor Company, to reverse his cancellation of a one million-dollar contract to sponsor *Combat* and *Stoney Burke* in January 1963.

Frawley, a staunch supporter of Dr. Fred Schwarz, director of the Christian Anti-Communism Crusade, had sent ABC the cancellation telegram Wednesday, November 14, 1962, in response to the appearance of Alger Hiss on Howard K. Smith's news program "The Political Obituary of Richard M. Nixon," which analyzed Nixon's recent defeat in the California governor's race.

In 1948, Alger Hiss, a former State Department official, had been convicted of perjury during his testimony before the House Un-American Activities Committee, of which Nixon was a member. Hiss had denied his participation in a Communist spy ring and been found guilty of lying. On the Smith program, Hiss accused Nixon of being "politically carried along" and of "molding appearances to a point of view that he began with" during the HUAC investigations in the late 1940s.

Following Hiss's appearance on the program, a contradictory view was presented by Gerald R. Ford Jr., then a Republican congressman from Michigan. Ford said that "the American people owe a great deal to Dick Nixon for his dedication to finding out all of the possible facts that the committee could find out about the Alger Hiss case and its ramifications."

The program in the fall of 1962 aired a couple of weeks after the Cuban Missile Crisis and the near nuclear showdown between the United States and the Soviet Union. The mood in America was strongly anti-Communist. Schick's telegram (the Schick Safety Razor Company had no connection with Schick, Inc., manufacturer of electric razors) seeking the cancellation stated that "we are shocked at the extreme poor taste and judgment shown by the ABC network in presenting a convicted perjurer involved in the passing of United States secrets to the Communists as a critic of the former Vice President of the U.S."

A number of ABC affiliates failed to carry the Smith program. Walter Annenberg, president of Triangle Publications and a close friend of Nixon's, ordered his two ABC affiliates, WFIL-TV in Philadelphia and WNHC-TV in New Haven, not to air the program.

Shortly after that, the Kemper Insurance Companies notified ABC of their decision to stop sponsorship of *ABC Evening Report*, a news program anchored by Ron Cochran, in violation of their contract.

This put ABC and the industry in the first major confrontation with advertisers' attempts to use economic coercion to influence editorial and news judgments. Other early attempts at influence in the past included similar encounters at CBS, described in Sally Bedell Smith's biography of William S. Paley, and some that occurred during the clashes between Edward R. Murrow and Sen. Joe McCarthy. I also recall a controversy about the American Gas Association's request to remove reference to gas chambers in the *Studio One* rendition of "The Nuremberg Trials."

ABC had problems early in its history with Walter Winchell's Sunday night programs. In 1958, ABC had to retract a charge made by Drew Pearson on Mike Wallace's Saturday night news program with respect to then Sen. John F. Kennedy's *Profiles in Courage*. Pearson alleged that Ted Sorenson, a Kennedy aide, and not the senator, was the author of the Pulitzer Prize–winning book. Kennedy and Clark Clifford convinced Leonard Goldenson that while bedridden for his chronic back injury, the senator had indeed created and drafted the chapters, which Sorenson then edited. Ollie Treyz went on the air to correct the mistake and apologize, but until the Smith incident no advertiser had attempted to influence news decisions in such a blatant manner.

ABC garnered support from the press and within the industry. The late Dick Salant, then president of CBS News, said he was "distressed at the pre-broadcast efforts to suppress any part of the Howard K. Smith broadcast and at the post broadcast actions by advertisers and others to punish ABC." He said such actions "struck at journalistic independence, including the right to be wrong and to present unpopular views."

The late LeRoy Collins, president of the NAB, said that the broadcast was within "the range of sound journalism," and Newton Minow, then chairman of the FCC, spoke out against advertisers who try to influence radio and television broadcast "through commercial reprisals."[3]

In the early 1960s, ABC could ill afford economic reprisals nor could it hope to build its own news department in an atmosphere hostile to journalistic integrity. Television news was in its infancy; CBS would air the first thirty-minute evening newscast in 1963. Hagerty, new to television, came from the newspaper business and had won accolades as an administrative aide and public spokesman for President Eisenhower.

On that 1962 L.A. trip, a policy was formulated about how to deal with special-interest groups and advertiser defections. The policy was to meet and talk with those who felt offended, frustrated, wronged, or misrepresented by our programming, news, or entertainment. It was also decided that though we wanted to learn from these dialogues, the network had to retain control.

Hagerty said,

> To yield to prior censorship and the pressure of personal attack and economic boycott is to surrender the basic right of freedom of the press. This right we will never surrender—or compromise. To do so would be to betray our responsibility as a news medium. If we are weakened, you [the public] are weakened, for if through fear or intimidation we fail to provide all the news—good or bad, favorable or unfavorable then you, the citizens of the nation cannot be properly informed.

That was what Hagerty and I said to Frawley in less formal terms. We advised him we would not let him out of his contract, which was our mission. We had also been told by management to listen and to explain our responsibilities in a democratic society to present balanced and objective news reports. And yes, the room to err in judgment as to what is newsworthy.

On November 15, 1962, after some eight hours of meetings, talk, breaking bread, shouting, and listening, Frawley issued a statement that his firm would live up to its legal commitments, but would do so reluctantly and under protest.

These efforts were the harbingers of future troubles. Our trip to Los Angeles to meet with Frawley was the first of many such meetings. As America underwent a revolution in lifestyles and politics, the controversial issues expanded beyond news programs into entertainment programming. In previous chapters, I examined those shifts in terms of violence and sexuality. With more issue-oriented programming and in the climate of protest and social ferment, special-interest groups soon targeted television in an effort to influence viewers.

I adapted the news policy to entertainment programs that came under fire from pressure groups. Their tactic at first was direct confrontation. Soon it evolved into attempts at economic boycott by encouraging viewers and constituents to pressure advertisers to withdraw sponsorship from television programs. Unlike newspapers, where commercials do not appear in the beginning, middle, and end of program content, the advertiser sometimes feels the association in a television program is inimical to his best interests.

Over the next thirty years, I would hear questions about taste, religion, style, politics—the entire spectrum of issues and concerns. Why did we not show more moments of religious observance such as grace at meals, prayers before bed? Why didn't we show the perversion of homosexual conduct, the sin of adultery? Why did we always show the big corporation as evil and the common man being taken advantage of? Why were most victims women? Why were there no positive role models, professionals who were black or Hispanic? When were we going to stop showing the Arabs in white sheets and burnoose as evil? Must the killer always be a psychopath and mental illness treated as leading to criminality? Why were the Polish people in *Winds of War* portrayed as participants in the atrocities at the Nazi concentration camps? Why can't Petula Clark kiss Harry Belafonte?

Every group, whatever the cause, believed they needed to set the record straight and to dictate television's treatment. The intent was to instruct the audience about what it should believe or feel about the issue or the group. It was a confusing and complex role for television. Where is that line between presentation of information and propaganda? A station's license was granted in the public interest, but exactly what did that require in action and programming? To me it meant inform, educate, but take no sides.

Such words as objectivity, fairness, balance, and equal opportunity were the guidelines, but each group had its own purpose and vision of how those words should be interpreted. What group did not feel itself misrepresented or stereotyped? While minorities pressed to expand the cast of characters on the nation's television screens, the "silent majority" voted its conviction that the news media had ignored the vast middle of the political spectrum.

One of the early abortive attempts to intimidate an advertiser occurred when *The Untouchables* was at the height of its popularity. The Italian-American leadership in New York City was concerned about depictions of Mafia characters as Italian-Americans. While meetings were held to discuss the problem, one afternoon I was summoned to Ollie Treyz's office and told to contact Albert Anastasia, a notorious labor leader, because longshoremen were dumping crates of Lucky Strike cigarettes off the docks. "Luckies" was a major sponsor of *The Untouchables*.

I need not tell you that at the age of thirty-five, starting a family of my own, I was not ready or prepared for a discussion with such a determined fellow as Mr. Anastasia. Saner heads prevailed. When we made it clear our discussions with the Italian-American leaders would end unless the dumping stopped, soon the longshoremen were reloading the cigarettes. In turn, ABC made a major concession not use the word Mafia on any future entertainment program. That commitment remained in effect until the early 1990s.

When advertisers began to purchase commercials in various programs throughout the schedule, so-called participation buys, rather than sponsor an entire program, we tried to convince advertisers that the "bonding" with a particular program was not as adhesive, but for many low-ticket items, the advertiser continued to worry about the image of his product and its connection with any type of controversy.

In the protest atmosphere fostered by the civil rights, antiwar, and women's movements, tactics learned from watching participants demonstrate on television news reports were adopted by many emerging pressure groups. In the early 1970s, one of the first and most vocal special-interest groups was the gay and lesbian community.

The explosive issue of how to depict gays and lesbians in television programs began shortly after the telecast of *That Certain Summer*, the first major television movie about homosexuality, which has been described in previous chapters. In January 1973, the New York–based Gay Activist Alliance, the precursor of the National Gay Task Force, brought the protest directly to ABC. Led by director Ron Gold, some twenty-five activists staged a sit-in in Leonard Goldenson's office on the thirty-ninth floor of the

ABC building on Sixth Avenue. Leonard had been out to lunch, and we were notified while in the executive dining room of their trespass.

The protest was over an episode of *Marcus Welby, M.D.*, the first of several programs that aroused ire in the gay community as it struggled for recognition and acceptance. Recently, homosexuals had won a victory from the American Psychiatric Association when homosexuality was removed from the list of mental illnesses. Leaders of the gay community now sought to use the media to state their case and to correct perceptions of homosexuality as deviant behavior.

Police were finally called and several protesters arrested after the group refused ABC's offer to meet with two of its representatives. Another *Welby* episode sparked more of a national protest. This resulted in an ABC relationship with the Gay Media Task Force, directed by Newt Dieter, a psychologist, in Los Angeles.

The first *Welby* episode, which concerned a married man seeking Welby's help in dealing with his homosexual tendencies, was broadcast with few changes. The second episode dealt with pedophilia, the molestation of a young teenage boy by a male schoolteacher. After much discussion, including suggestions made by our in-house consultant, Dr. Melvin Heller, the program made a clear distinction between the sex offender as someone with extreme emotional problems and homosexuality. All references to homosexuality were removed, and efforts were made to make the public, our affiliated stations, and the advertisers aware that this was not intended to be derogatory of homosexuality.

The homosexual community was not convinced; more protests and demonstrations followed. We continued the dialogue to assist us in an objective presentation of a homosexual character without taking sides in the religious and social controversy.

When BS&P tried to tone down what we perceived as a stereotypical gay character on *Barney Miller*, the long-running comedy about a New York police precinct, Danny Arnold blew up. Arnold, sympathetic to the homosexual community, felt that satire in comedy was not stereotyping. We, on the other hand, were in the middle of discussions with the gay community, who in fighting for their "cause," saw nothing funny in the portrayal.

The Family Viewing Hour controversy was under way, and the conflict with Arnold became ugly and hostile. BS&P also found ourselves in another no-win situation in the depiction of a homosexual on *Soap*. This character managed to offend both sides of the controversy: the religious community saw the Billy Crystal character as proselytizing for homosexual acceptance, and the gay community was offended by Crystal's over-the-top performance.

Soap, first telecast in the fall of 1977 on Tuesdays at 9:30 P.M. EST and discussed in an earlier chapter, probably raised more ire than any other series previously broadcast and gave the religious right a platform for protest and pressure. The depiction of sexual activity and sexual content was at the heart of the campaigns and threatened boycotts launched first by the Moral Majority and later the Reverend Mr. Wildmon.

The Reverend Jerry Falwell's role as prime spokesman for the fundamentalist special-interest groups was taken over in the 1980s by the Reverend Donald Wildmon from Tupelo, Mississippi. First through a group called Christian Leaders for Responsible Television and later the American Family Association, he called for consumer boycotts of advertisers who sponsored shows containing sex, violence, and profanity. The creative community became extremely concerned. They feared how these threats might affect their programs and profits.

In 1981, at the urging of David Wolper and other leaders in the entertainment community, the Academy of Television Arts and Sciences and the Caucus of Writers, Producers and Directors convened a symposium in Ojai, California. The purpose was "develop[ing] more thoughtful and coherent means of responding to the pressure groups, so that we may learn from our critics while resisting censorship."

In essence, the mission was to support the networks and advertisers without "blanding out" the medium. Conclusions were reached, namely, that diversity of thought is healthy, pressure groups are O.K., but their methods are unacceptable, and that stations and networks should have guidelines to deal with their complaints and be strictly enforced.

Advertisers responded by setting up along with their agencies screening services. These services would screen every prime-time program and report back to the agency or the advertiser matters that the screener believed in any way might cause a special-interest group to object. The advertiser or his agency representative would then contact the sales department of the network and ask to be moved out of the program or relieved of sponsorship. In most instances, the commercial could be replaced with that of another advertiser, but it invariably led to a loss of revenue for the network. Although advertisers realized that the boycott attempts produced insignificant results, not much impact on the purchasing of products, they simply did not want to have the negative publicity associated with their company or image. The actual "chilling effect" is difficult to measure in real terms, but possibly affected programs that were not highly successful.

In January 1984, ABC finally published a workbook entitled *Sexuality, Television and Broadcast Standards,* as a supplement to *Broadcast Standards &*

Editing issued in 1978. This guide was written by Dr. Heller, our respected friend and valued colleague. Heller had discussed the topic at length with our BS&P editors. He also conferred with Dr. Philip Sarrel and Ms. Lorna Sarrel, Yale professors and consultants to ABC about the consequences, emotional impact, and societal perceptions of proposed sexual content in our programming. The result set forth our policy and guideline for handling the question of homosexual behavior. That monograph also served as our effort to codify our practices in reviewing all programming dealing with sexuality.

Over the years, whatever the cause of alarm, sexuality, violence, or minority misrepresentation, it's doubtful any program popular with the public was injured by threats or protests. For example, when Ms. Terry Rekolta spoke out about the concern she had with her children viewing *Married with Children*, then a leading-edge sexually oriented situation comedy on the new Fox network, sponsors reacted, but the program made very few if any creative changes and continued to draw a significant audience.

Ms. Rekolta gained visibility and began her own protest organization, "Americans for Responsible Television," which joined the outcry against the radio disc jockey Howard Stern, who was charged with violating the new indecency rules promulgated by the FCC. In the latter part of the 80s, the FCC, in response to congressional pressure and conservative outcry, much of it induced by the fundamentalist right, adopted the Pacifica ruling (the seven dirty words), which applied to radio lyrics and talk shows and imposed fines upon broadcasters who carried what was deemed indecent material.

At times, during the past thirty years, television and newspaper reports have promoted the rhetoric of passion and anger instead of reason. The media, which has expanded in number and reach, gives the forces of intimidation undue attention. By overreporting the size and actual strength of any movement, the impact is exaggerated and can trigger an excessive reaction. We should be able to depend upon the press not to take political and social happenings out of context, but too often these days competitive pressures produce an emphasize on speed and not accuracy and in-depth analysis.

The broadcaster must not only be concerned about political pressures from the Right and the Left, but also be wary of those who attempt to use the medium for "public service" propaganda. The medium needs to give the public the choice on issues and values facing society, free of undisclosed influence and pressure from those who would impose their particular cause or humanistic values on others.

Some examples are the "Don't Drink and Drive" campaign, advocated by the Harvard School of Public Health, which made a direct approach to producers to include in program content the theme of "use of a designated driver" or the late President Nixon's asking for the inclusion of content explicitly dealing with the tragedies and illegalities of drug abuse. The television version of "idea placement" is more insidious than product placements in the movies.

In the summer of 1992, executives from the three television networks were invited to a workshop under the auspices of the Humanitas Committee, a group headed by a Roman Catholic priest, the Reverend Ellwood Kaiser, to discuss how to make programs more "humanly enriching"— more of "family values," traditional institutions, marriage, the home, sex. Promises were made to introduce these qualities in television programs. I disagreed. It is one thing to agree to inform and educate, another to commit.

A program celebrating Earth Day in 1992 required diligence in balancing environmental interests with economic and commercial business and employment considerations. We sought to avoid overstatement of the arguments for conservation, pollution control, and recycling without countervailing considerations.

Late in 1999 it came to light that the networks had agreed to trade mentions of antidrug messages in program content for credit from the government for public-service time obligations pursuant to certain legislation—a practice I would not have agreed to and one that was quickly reversed by the networks after media disclosure.

Clearly, a rationale dialogue must be maintained with special-interest groups, and I often felt I talked with a representative of almost every imaginable issue: children, sexuality, ethnicity, stereotyping, civil rights, mental health, drug addition, animals, the family, guns, even water beds. Given the pervasiveness of the medium, the sheer volume of television programming, and its impact on society, it is no wonder that television attracts advocates, but it is not television's role to redress grievances, halt crime on the streets, reduce divorce rates, or feed the hungry. Although it can raise the consciousness of the nation, it is not the vehicle for relief or altering behavior. The ultimate choice must remain with the viewer. To achieve this objective, the commitment must be to diversity, fairness, and balance.

How ironic that sometimes those who would inhibit speech owe their voice to the core principle of free speech! This somewhat blind view makes it necessary to be vigilant against threats to free speech. Without contrasting and sometimes contrary voices, we risk blandness and boredom, maybe even totalitarianism. There is no surer route to decadence and self-destruction than the exercise of repressive control over thought.

We are a nation of a majority of minorities. In such a pluralistic society, meaningful dialogue, rational discourse, is the sine qua non for divergent groups to express genuine concerns. Those in power, whether in charge of the government or the media, need to hear diverse voices. Viewers must have an outlet for their frustrations created by messages constantly projected at them.

Special-interest groups cannot be allowed to superimpose their wills, their standards, their special objectives and goals any more than the broadcaster can allow the creative community, an advertiser, or even the broadcaster to impose special concerns on television programming.

Television, especially broadcast television, with its network of local affiliates, will remain a focus of special-interest groups. In some ways, despite the loss of market share, the splintered media landscape makes television an even more recognizable target of opportunity. I believe the industry has a responsibility to continue to meet, talk, and listen, and to respond and change. Attitudes and values change; the effort to balance points of view, to be as objective as possible, requires a continual effort. Perhaps the best way to describe the process is an effort to enlighten as well as entertain the audience.

"The Family Viewing Hour"

In the fall of 1974, that familiar refrain "do something about violence on television," which appeared soon after the first sets were introduced in America's living rooms and resounds after any especially violent episode in the news, became an outcry loud enough to stir up Congress to threaten action, not just more hearings.

Why then?

In the 1960s and early 1970s, the nation watched civil rights marches, assassinations, antiwar protests, the Vietnam War, the emergence of various special-interest groups, and the breakup of traditional values and mores; television came in for both praise and blame for its role in these cataclysmic changes.

By the midpoint of the 1970s, programming reflected the new social realities, and the portrayals of violence became more graphic. *Gunsmoke* and traditional action-adventure programs gave way to more aggressive, city-street violence in such programs as *The Rookies, Police Story, Kolchak: The Night Stalker, Police Woman,* and *S.W.A.T.,* and the number of action programs also increased. *All in the Family, Maude, The Jeffersons,* and *M*A*S*H* broke new comedic ground in topics and treatment of social issues.

In the television industry, the new guard, represented by young Hollywood turks eager to tap the potential of a young, hip audience, encouraged bright and innovative concepts that "pushed the envelope." The managers and owners of affiliate stations, the first to hear and feel public pressure, were more traditional, wary of change, and responsive to complaints from parents. Operating under government licenses, the affiliates heard complaints and urgent requests "to do something," even when the national agenda focused on other issues.

Members of Congress, also more traditional, heard from anxious parents and uneasy constituents. The FCC, which regulated the industry, received a flood of complaints. In late summer 1974, Richard Nixon resigned as president, ending the long national preoccupation with Watergate. Headlines and bloody newscasts from Vietnam disappeared as the war moved toward its unhappy end the following spring. Inflation was up. America now dealt with the aftermath of its social and political revolution. The stage was set.

"The Family Viewing Hour" that eventually resulted was as much about what had happened to America as it was about what was shown on television. The issue met its moment at a unique time in broadcasting history, when the three networks still controlled most of the programming for all of the nation.

The FCC, which was scheduled to seek renewed funding from the Appropriations Committee, heard directly from senators and representatives who wanted answers for their constituents. The mandate, not official, but determined, was there: "do something."

Many business and opinion leaders also voiced their concerns about the impact television violence would have on the behavior of young children. Others complained about moral laxity in programming.

Television again became the nation's favorite scapegoat. About to face the Appropriations Committee, FCC commissioner Richard Wiley sought out the three network chiefs to provide response to the criticism, to offer some evidence of industry self-regulation and responsibility. Wiley understood First Amendment limits, knew he could not be specific in his request, but he came with the specter of possible congressional action.

I believed ABC was in the best position to give a responsible answer. BS&P had conducted a series of clinical and interrogatory studies on the effect of TV violence on children. We had published a handbook, "Broadcast Standards Editing," which set forth stringent guidelines and principles for violent programs as well as programs designed for children. Dr. Heller was at work on a handbook dealing with sexual matters, which would explain inhibitions, actions, ignorance, and fear, and suggest ways to deal with sexual topics without sensationalism.

CBS had no written policy. NBC did have written guidelines, but was in a precarious position because of the recent telecast of *Born Innocent,* a two-hour drama involving the graphic portrayal of a sexual assault. NBC was under fire from advertisers and affiliates after an alleged copycat assault took place in San Francisco. With such a public outcry, NBC was too vulnerable to defend the ability of the industry to self-police.

Into this cauldron of competitive interests, confrontations between old and new values, and the complex web of industry and government relations came Arthur Taylor, president of CBS, with his suggestion that the in-

dustry adopt a provision that would embody "the three general principles" reflected in CBS's belief that (1) programming in the first hour of the
network prime-time schedule be suitable for family viewing, (2) when a
"special" represents an exception to the appropriate-for-family-viewing
criterion, a notice be broadcast to facilitate parental guidance, and (3) in
other viewing hours provide advance notice when material that might be
disturbing to a significant portion of the adult audience is being presented.

I opposed for competitive and administrative reasons an industry rule
based on the idea of a "safe harbor." I thought ABC had control of its programming, because of our standards operation and relationships with
producers.

For example, I had a good working, mutually respectful relationship
with Aaron Spelling, producer of *The Rookies.* Aaron was a brilliant writer
who had the pulse of the audience and a keen sense of how to move a sixty-
minute drama. He knew just how far he could push me, and when he tried
to push the envelope, he would call and plead his case. Many times we
compromised and found ways to create what he wanted within prescribed
limits. He would use stop-action, have an act occur off-camera, or trade a
blow for a gunshot—never with malice but always to achieve a creative
edge. I admired and respected his ingenuity; he knew I had a job to do and
often found a way to get me off the hook.

We didn't need a third party to second-guess our subtle negotiations,
and that applied to other relationships between BS&P editors and producers of ABC programming. The job of editor – censor—is not, as commonly
perceived, to wield scissors or a blue pencil. In a world of competition and
innovation, an editor must understand the creative purpose, appreciate
the dramatic or creative form, and work with a sense of responsibility.

The standards editor operates from a unique position: a desire to see
the product succeed without excess or sensationalism. The goal is to balance the excitement of storytelling with respect for the emotions and perceptions of the viewers. Broadcasters are licensed to operate "in the public
interest" of those viewers.

A series of meetings about what the television industry would and
could do in this atmosphere of public and governmental pressure culminated in a historic meeting of the National Association of Broadcasters
Code Review Board on January 7, 1975, where CBS had gotten Wayne
Kearl of San Antonio, chairman of the Code Review Board, to put its proposal for a Family Viewing Hour on the agenda.

United in our desire to stave off government action, each network had
separate agendas, based on competitive realities and concerns. As noted
earlier, ABC and NBC, both with written guidelines in operation, wanted

independent statements of policy and standards to suffice; CBS led the charge for an industrywide response.

At CBS, Taylor, who had a strong financial background, had been brought in by William Paley as his successor. In my view, Taylor's proposal came out of his strong concerns about the effect of violent portrayals on society. I also believe he was not as disturbed about the treatment of sexual issues, and had struck up a cordial relationship with Norman Lear. Taylor sought a means to regulate programming, but not one that would put CBS at a competitive disadvantage.

Perhaps because Taylor did not have total operating management support or because he saw competitive dangers to each network operating under a similar policy, but subject to independent judgment, he sent his generals into that acrimonious and decisive battle.

If Tom Swafford, the CBS representative, could get the Code Review Board to adopt a policy of "unsuitable for family viewing before 9 P.M.," CBS could produce change without suffering competitive harm. Swafford and CBS had no program portraying graphic violence in the eight-to-nine time period, because a Western such as *Gunsmoke* was not an issue.

The meeting led to what a federal judge in a later ruling described as "an inelegant display of competitive fervor." In Judge Warren Ferguson's decision, I am quoted as saying to Swafford, "Well, if you are not going to move the goddamn program 'All in the Family,' we are not going to move the goddamn 'Rookies.' " In my notes, I did not recall use of profanity; however, Judge Ferguson's characterization that the meeting "ultimately disintegrated into a shouting match over the potential application of the Family Hour" was accurate.

ABC stood to lose the most. *The Rookies* at eight o'clock Monday night was a dominant winner in our schedule. Although NBC and ABC were prepared to accept the principle of family viewing, implementation created the dilemma. Who was going to judge whether or not a violation was about to occur or had occurred? Why, and in whose judgment, was *The Rookies* to be deemed more unsuitable for 8 P.M. viewing than *All in the Family?* The two programs became the icons of violence and sex.

As to *The Rookies*, I believed we had invoked appropriate standards limiting violent portrayal. We applied guidelines of human consequences, infusion of humor, and no detailed descriptions or visuals of "how to" commit a unique act of crime in a unique detailed way. On the other hand, Laura Z. Hobson, author of *Gentleman's Agreement*, a groundbreaking book/movie about anti-Semitism, had insisted in a lengthy article, published in the *New York Times*, September 1971, that *All in the Family*, contrary to Norman Lear's position, did reinforce bigotry, a subject certainly inap-

propriate for young minds, not to mention other sexual topics. I had recommended rejection of *All in the Family* when it was being considered as a
pilot for ABC, because of its sexual content.

The only agreement from that historic meeting was to meet again. The
next day, January 8, before another Wiley meeting with the networks, ABC
issued a policy statement to the public:

> The American Broadcasting Company acknowledges and accepts the
> continuing responsibility to its viewers for all programs broadcast by the
> ABC Television Network. We are, and have been, aware of our obligation
> to select, with sensitivity, programs cognizant of the possible effect that vi-
> olence and certain adult themes may have on that audience, particularly
> younger viewers.
>
> Aware of current public opinion concerns and in order to better in-
> form the viewing audience, ABC has been televising audio and video ad-
> visory announcements, when appropriate, in certain entertainment
> programs to afford parents the opportunity to exercise discretion in re-
> gard to younger viewers.
>
> As part of a continuing review of these policies, we have recently in-
> creased the use of such audio-visual viewer advisories, and will also now
> be including them in print advertising and on-air promotional material.
>
> As an additional measure, starting with the new television season in
> the Fall of 1975, the first hour of each night of the week of our prime time
> network entertainment schedule will be devoted to programming suit-
> able for general family audiences. When in our judgment, programming
> in this period may, on occasion, contain material which might be regarded
> as unsuitable for younger members of the family, the audience will be ap-
> propriately advised as outlined above.
>
> We wish to emphasize the necessity to preserve the basic rights of free-
> dom of expression under the Constitution and under the Communications
> Act. Government action in the area of program content must be both cau-
> tious and carefully limited lest we do permanent damage to the principles
> of free expression which are so fundamental in our society. All Americans
> recognize, we are sure, that these are sensitive and fragile concepts. Ac-
> cordingly, ABC strongly supports the concept of industry self-regulation.
>
> The providing of network television programming is an extremely
> complicated task which we attempt to do in a responsible fashion. We
> serve a diverse audience, among whom are people with wide differences
> of opinion about our programs. For instance, there are those who look
> upon the treatment of certain subjects in dramatic programs as too contro-
> versial to be touched upon. There are also those who feel that these same
> subjects reflect changes in our society which television should realistically
> portray; and if not, has failed its responsibility. It is for these reasons that

we attempt to present each season a balanced program schedule with diverse content and program types which will appeal to broad segments of the public.

Violence

Since June of 1968, the following has been the policy of American Broadcasting Company with respect to portrayal of violence in television programs:

The use of violence for the sake of violence is prohibited. In this connection, special attention should be given to encourage the de-emphasis of acts of violence.

While a story-line or plot development may call for the use of force—the amount, manner of portrayal and necessity for same should be commensurate with a standard of reasonableness and with due regard for the principle that violence, or the use of force, as an appropriate means to an end, is not to be emulated.

Additionally, special attention has been directed to avoid close-ups of demonstrations of criminal techniques. The foregoing has been brought to the attention of producers of ABC entertainment programs on a regular basis.

It has also been ABC's policy, since April, 1972, to prohibit acts of personal violence from being portrayed in teasers, prologues and promotional announcements.

In connection with the application of this policy and because of our special concerns over the possible effects of televised violence on young people, ABC took the initiative to sponsor on-going research in this area and has retained two teams of entirely independent research consultants. An important adjunct to this research is the refinement and continued development of guidelines by which we can effectuate our policies. We have found, for example, that violence can be responsibly portrayed to the extent to which its consequences are adequately depicted in depth. Under these circumstances, such portrayals may have even had the effect of reinforcing real-life prohibitions, thereby acting as a suppressor of violence. On the other hand, as it is clear that gratuitous violence serves no useful purpose and may be emulated, we are extremely cautious in avoiding the portrayal of specific, detailed techniques involved in the use of weapons, the commission of crimes or avoidance of detection.

Adult Subject Matter

In meeting the challenge to present innovative programming which deals with significant moral or social issues and with current topical program treatment of inter-personal relationships, it has been a guiding principle that the presentation of such material be accomplished without exploitation, unsensationally and responsibly. In relation to made-for-television programs it is the responsibility of the Standards and Practices Department to review material which includes sensitive or controversial matter from the script stage through the final print so as to avoid the exploitative and sensational.

Feature films initially produced by others for theatrical release are screened prior to acquisition by ABC to determine, in the first instance, the acceptability of the overall theme and tenor of the films and, if appropriate, in the second instance, the nature and extent of editing which we will require to assure compliance with our policies. After acquisition the films are screened again to review prior judgments, and as an additional measure, the edited version is viewed prior to telecast to insure compliance with broadcast standards and practices directives. In the event a film which we proposed to televise was originally rated "R," we required that it be resubmitted to the Motion Picture Association of America for reclassification in terms of their judgment and on the basis of our editing. If the MPAA feels that the edits would have made the picture presentable theatrically with a higher rating than "R," e.g., "PG" or "G," we will then accept it for telecast.

As a matter of practice ABC follows the following procedures:

1. Advisory announcements, when made, are commonly telecast in the following form: "This film deals with mature subject matter. Parental judgment and discretion are advised."

2. All affiliates are furnished Advance Program Advisory bulletins detailing content.

3. Closed circuit previews of prime time programs are presented on a regularly scheduled rotational basis.

4. Advance descriptive program information is made available to the NAB Code Authority and the NAB Code Authority Director is accorded an opportunity to request screenings prior to broadcast. All pilot programs are prescreened for the NAB Code Authority Director.

5. Our independent outside consultants (Dr. Melvin Heller and Dr. Samuel Polsky) review all pilots and other programming from time to time as requested by the Standards and Practices Department.

The foregoing policies will continue to be implemented by our Department of Broadcast Standards and Practices in consultation with ABC's independent consultants.

At a January 9 meeting with Wiley, ABC and NBC management again advocated independent approaches. When CBS stated that its proposal did not contemplate any external or other outside authority making prejudgments, or condone prescreening on the suitability of a program for family viewing, NBC caved and agreed to support an industrywide policy. The mechanics of implementation would be a posttelecast procedure to be worked out by the Code Board.

The die was cast. The Program Standards Committee of the Code Board was directed to meet January 28 to try again to formulate policy and procedure for NAB adoption of a family viewing policy. Here is the result of that session, again as summarized by Judge Ferguson, who eventually presided over the lawsuit brought by the production community, in his findings of fact:

The Committee was composed of the three network representatives, Swafford (CBS), Schneider (ABC) and Hermino Traviesas (NBC) together with Rich, the representative from the Duluth, NBC affiliate. The Committee wrangled and fought and could not agree to do anything more than pass a resolution: "Because several constructive proposals were proffered as to the approach to be taken by the Television Code Review Board in response to the NAB Television Board of Directors' resolution, the Program Standards Committee recommends that the same be presented to the full Television Code Review Board for its review and resolution." That innocuous resolution masked a bitter set of differences. CBS, of course, was very much in favor of NAB Code enforcement. Both NBC and ABC were opposed to NAB enforcement but were willing to support some type of NAB statement of principle. ABC favored a resolution which would have provided in part that during "the first hour of network entertainment programming in prime time and in the immediately preceding hour, broadcasters devote their schedules to programming suitable for general family audiences." The principles declared in the resolution would not be enforced under the NAB Code but instead the NAB would "use its leadership to further the objectives of this policy in encouraging industry-wide adherence."

NBC proposed that language be placed in a "Supplement" to the Code: Entertainment programming inappropriate for viewing by family audiences should not be broadcast during early evening time periods, including the first hour of network prime-time programming. The NBC proposal similarly eschewed NAB enforcement. "[T]he suitability of programming to time periods . . . are matters for judgment solely by the broadcaster on a case-by-case basis." Thus both ABC and NBC were unwilling to delegate their authority to make programming decisions to outside authority. Schneider put it crisply, "I don't want [Code Authority director] Stockton Helffrich programming our network."

Swafford responded by pointing out that "[A]ll of us had surrendered that kind of authority to the Code Authority in subscribing to the Code." The discussion evolved, as had the January 7 Code Board meeting, into a battle over specifics.

Schneider pressed Swafford to tell what CBS planned to do with "All In The Family." Once again Schneider warned that if CBS did not move "All In The Family," ABC would not move the "Rookies." As Swafford points out, by this point the two shows had become "shorthand for sex and violence." They had become symbols of broadcaster good faith in applying the family viewing concept. But in keeping with CBS' strategy, Swafford refused to discuss the application of the policy.

Rich emerged at the meeting as a critic of each of the network policies. He announced that he was dead set against government intrusion. He criticized the fact that the proposal as applied in the Midwest would be applicable from 6–8 P.M. instead of 7–9 P.M. (because of the feed in from New York) and did not see how the networks could justify a protective policy which did not apply to one third of the nation's children.

Swafford's recollection of the exchanges at the Meeting was that [it] was almost "vicious", "the only thing we could agree on at today's meeting . . . was that we could not agree."

Besides the question of who decided which programs complied to the policy, another concern that I shared with our affiliates was why establish a Family Viewing Hour, the so-called safe harbor for networks, in that first prime-time hour, when independent stations could program without restriction.

Another obvious question was about programming in access time from 7 to 8 P.M. Could a network affiliate or independent station show a syndicated *The Mod Squad* or other action program in that time period, or schedule *All in the Family* when it became available for syndication when similar programs would not be suitable during the Family Hour? To answer that question, I proposed and secured agreement to include the hour immediately preceding the first hour of network prime-time programming. This provision later caused the Independent Television Association to seek a grandfather provision, because they felt extension of the Family Viewing policy put independent stations at a competitive disadvantage.

Another Code Board meeting was held in February 1975, before Wiley was to appear before Congress to report on his efforts to contain violence. At that meeting, ABC and NBC strongly advocated individual policy statements that would leave implementation to each network, with perhaps an informal review from time to time at Code Review Board meetings. The impact of FCC jawboning, political expediency, Taylor's apprehension about the effect of each network going it alone (at one point, Swafford on behalf of CBS threatened to withdraw from the code if nothing was passed), and the unknown thinking of the independent stations dictated a policy statement. The need for closure and a desire to put it all behind us gave birth to the Family Viewing Policy.

It stated:

> Entertainment programming inappropriate for viewing by a general family audience should not be broadcast during the first hour of network entertainment programming in prime time and in the immediately preceding hour. In the occasional case when an entertainment program in this time period is deemed to be inappropriate for such an audience, advisories should be used to alert viewers. Advisories should also be used when programs in later prime time periods contain material that might be disturbing to significant segments of the audience.
>
> These advisories should be presented in audio and video from the beginning of the program and when deemed appropriate at a later point in the program. Advisories should also be used responsibly in promotional material in advance of the program. When using an advisory, the broadcaster should attempt to notify publishers of television program listings.
>
> Special care should be taken with respect to the content and treatment of audience advisories so that they do not deserve their intended purpose by containing material that is promotional, sensational or exploitative. Promotional announcements for programs that include advisories should be scheduled on a basis consistent with the purpose of the advisory.[1]

The proposal went to the full board of the NAB at its April meeting and was passed. This left creation of an operating procedure to a future Code Board meeting. A rancorous winter and spring were ahead.

ABC held meetings with affiliates, who had mixed reactions. Some supported the policy because they believed there was too much violence on the airwaves and saw this action as a means of curtailment. Others opposed the policy as a loss of their independence and ability to act individually.

We met several times with the late Stockton Hellfrich, director of the Code Authority, trying to devise a procedure that would eliminate a surrogate decision-maker in our dealings with producers. This was a critical point for us, because in the fragile relationship of censor and producer, much depends upon goodwill and personal relationships. Often, the power to negotiate a compromise depends upon the support of both programming department executives and management. The introduction of a third party's subjective view, certainly at the script stage, would be totally unmanageable.

In our producers meeting that summer, producers made us keenly aware of their distaste for another "policy" and restriction. They also were concerned about another "voice" with which to negotiate.

In October 1975, the Code Board met and with much blood, sweat, and tears, the following implementation procedure was agreed to:

If the Code authority received a challenge from "any source" with respect to a prime time family viewing program:

1. The challenge should be referred to the originating network or station.

2. The network or station will answer the challenger in writing, sending a carbon of the response to the Code Authority Director.

3. If the challenger disagrees with the response of the network or station, the Code Authority Director, upon receipt of a request from the challenger will review the matter. If the Code Authority Director agrees with the challenger, the network or station may seek review of the issue by the Programs Standard Committee of the Board.

4. The challenger may request an appearance before the full Television Code Review Board to review the matter if the Committee's response is not satisfactory to him/her.

The code itself provided that the Code Board had the authority to "consider, in its discretion, any appeal from any decision made by the Code Authority Director" (NAB, The Television Code 30 [18th ed., 1975]).

Besides creating a system that would allow challenges from any source to be considered by the Code Authority, the Code Authority itself undertook an extensive monitoring process. The heart of the matter, what constituted a breach of the Family Viewing Policy, was left ambiguous. We had tentatively set the limits in our discussion with *Rookies* for violence and *All in the Family* for language and sex, but no specifics. Nothing.

Hellfrich, in an internal memo to his Code Review Board staff about the monitoring procedure, stated that "it would be complicated by the fact that the Television Code Review Board had not established criteria designed to help determine whether or not a program, or part thereof, scheduled in the seven to nine p.m. EST slot conforms to the 'family viewing concept.' " Rather than formulate "rigid definitions," Hellfrich proposed that the members of the staff proceed by "trial and error," and so they did.

We had won an illusory victory in forestalling a before-telecast, prescreening by the Code Authority. We would apply our own judgment and see what happened. If called to account for a "failure" by the Code Board, we would have to apply the results to future script and tape reviews of a program. Just such an incident resulted in the most excruciating moments of my career.

In September 1975, ABC telecast a two-hour movie of the week entitled *Mobile Two,* which contained a number of *hell*s and *damn*s in the dialogue.

After its telecast, Hellfrich sent us a letter expressing his monitor's concern about the extent to which language may have violated family viewing standards. He stated that the use of the words *hell* and *damn*, in the particular context, was "code-compliant," but warned that "from the Code Board itself I estimate a majority sentiment in respect to uses of words such as 'damn,' and 'hell,' [in programs in the Prime Time Family Programming time periods] as best *generally* eschewed, and when and if employed, used only with rare exception and strictly where appropriate."

We took his admonishment seriously. The use of *hell*s and *damn*s raised heck in the hinterland, and affiliated station managers from Kansas to Missouri to Utah and Illinois told us so.

After many attempts at getting a series on the networks, Danny Arnold finally struck it rich with *Barney Miller* in the winter of 1975. This humorous, satirical, well-written, and superbly acted comedy/drama took place primarily in a precinct house in New York City. With diverse characters, poignancy, and wit, Arnold dealt with themes that involved sex and violence, and lifestyles that did not find general acceptance or familiarity in middle America. Danny wanted the program to remain street-smart, reality-oriented, and cutting-edge in language and subject matter.

In anticipation of Family Viewing problems with the renewal of *Barney Miller* at 8 P.M. Thursday, I visited Arnold in late May, 1975, to advise him of how we would implement the policy. I told him I thought his story lines dealing with Marty, a gay character and young prostitute, used as a foil for the straight and narrow rural detective Wojeckowski, played so well by Max Gale, would have to go. Aware of Hellfrich's warning concerning the use of *hell*s and *damn*s, I reiterated my concern with his excessive use of those words. Neither word bothered the audience in urban viewing areas such as New York, Chicago, or Los Angeles, but raised the ire of conservatives in the heartland and among religious fundamentalists.

When I raised these matters with Arnold, he became hostile and refused to cooperate. This made my job all the more difficult at a time when we had yet to determine what was or was not acceptable to the Code Authority, and I became just as hostile. War was declared one day in August, when I visited the set unannounced. We challenged each other face to face for the last time.

Geoffrey Cowan, in his book on the family viewing case, *See No Evil,* gives a more vivid and colorful description of that encounter as apparently reported by the late Danny Arnold.[2] It fails, however, to relate my struggle to deal with a policy that did not take context into consideration.

Outside forces, those unhappy with changing mores and behavior, used application of the "family viewing concept" to assuage their ire with the medium and its introduction of previously taboo subjects such as homosexuality and prostitution. Arnold, on the other hand, was offended by the intrusion into his creative territory and apparent infringement upon his freedom of expression. The first show of the new season was taped with the line "You know, you've got one hell of a nerve"; when it was viewed by our editor, Arnold was told the show could not air unless he changed "hell" to "heck." Arnold fought vigorously but finally agreed to dub the line.

At CBS, Tom Swafford was not having it any easier with Norman Lear and *All in the Family*. Lear did not want *All in the Family* moved from its successful spot at eight o'clock Saturday night. Lear also resented interference with his creativity, freedom, and sense of good taste, and refused to make many of the changes that would be required to keep the show in that time period.

In a memo to CBS president Robert Wood, Swafford summarized his position and the dilemma we all faced. Dealing with whether or not *All in the Family* should run during the family viewing time or be moved to a later time period, Swafford wrote:

> I believe Stockton Helffrich would rule that it is [acceptable for family viewing]. However, machinery is being set up which could automatically take all "family viewing decisions" by the Code Authority Director to the full Code Review Board. . . . Knowing the makeup of that Board, knowing how they resisted this concept, knowing how they grudgingly came around to our point of view; along with the awareness that from the very beginning of our deliberations "All in The Family" was repeatedly used as shorthand for what is not family viewing . . . with all this I'm quite certain that the Board would rule against us.[3]

Then, despite the fact that Swafford thought the moving of *All in the Family* was "unpalatable" and "goes down hard," he saw no other alternative but to move the show. "[W]ould we—could we, really—ignore the Code? I think that one answers itself."

At NBC, Herminio Traviesas experienced similar battles with Susan Harris and Paul Witt over the sexy sophisticated barrier-breaking program *Fay*, a comedy about a divorced woman, played by Lee Grant, and her escapades.

In the fall of 1975, ABC moved *The Rookies* to nine o'clock on Tuesday night, where it played as strong as ever. New guidelines were promulgated for *The Six Million Dollar Man*, decreasing its violent content, cautioning on too much slow motion (to avoid detailed depiction of violence), and adding pro-social aspects to retain its 8:30 P.M. period.

In November 1975, two months after the fall season began, unhappy producers took their case to court. Norman Lear, Danny Arnold, Larry Gelbart, other independent producers, and the Writers Guild of America challenged the NAB's Family Viewing Policy as an infringement of First Amendment rights, and sought damages. The case was filed in a federal district court in California.

One year later, November 1976, Judge Ferguson, found that the adoption of the Family Viewing Policy violated the First Amendment prohibition against abridging freedom of speech and was unconstitutional.[3] Although the court agreed that private parties generally may lawfully restrain speech, the judge found the networks and the NAB had acted in collaboration with the government, represented by the FCC, which gave their actions the mantle of government authority. The court went on to say that the networks were free to continue or discontinue the Family Viewing Policy as long as their decisions were based on their independent conceptions of the public interest. The court refused Norman Lear's request that CBS be ordered to move *All in The Family* back to 8 P.M.

The threat of legislation ever present, each network independently appealed the decision and reaffirmed public commitment to the policy. Acting on legal advice, ABC, as did the other networks, discontinued sending advance descriptive programming information to the NAB Code Authority, suspended NAB screenings of ABC programs, either before or after broadcast, and refused to attend Code Board meetings. In effect, the days of the Code Board's involvement in programming matters were over.

Three years later, November 1979, the Court of Appeals for the Ninth Circuit declared the primary jurisdiction for deciding the constitutionality of the Family Viewing Policy was the FCC, not a federal district court in California. It vacated the lower court's decision and remanded the case with instruction "to refer plaintiffs' claims against government defendants (Wiley, et al) to the FCC and to hold in abeyance the claims against the networks pending resolution and judicial review of the Administrative proceedings before the FCC."

Throughout the early 1980s, the case traveled back through the FCC, and finally on September 23, 1983, some eight years after the birth of the Family Viewing Policy, the FCC released a report in which it concluded that it had acted lawfully:

> After careful consideration of the plaintiffs' claims against the FCC and the seven named commissioners, the record adduced in the district court, the decision of the district court and the court of appeals, as well as the comments filed upon remand [sic] at our request, we have concluded

that the actions which formed the basis of the complaints against the Commission's former chairman and the other commissioners named in the complaint were neither unlawful nor improper. The record developed in the district court makes clear to us that the NAB family viewing policy was not the child of coercion exercised by former Chairman Wiley or the Commission. Rather, the record supports the conclusion that the decision to adopt the family viewing amendment, although undoubtedly motivated by a variety of relevant considerations, was the result of a voluntary decision by the three commercial television networks, the NAB, and the NAB Code Review Board. (report, p. 2)

The report was nothing more than a legal footnote. By 1983, the television landscape had been changed dramatically by cable, satellites, and VCRs, which gave programming, adult movies, and so on, to the viewer's control. On cable, movies originally made for theatrical distribution aired unedited and without commercials in time slots once designated for "family viewing." Network entertainment programs continued to expand the definitions of what was acceptable in language and content.

In May 1984, a settlement was reached by the networks and plaintiffs disposing of the case in its entirety, including the First Amendment claim. The settlement came two years after the death of the code in a Justice Department consent decree, which resolved certain antitrust issues regarding industrywide advertising standards.

The NAB Code Authority and the dominance of the three networks that had made such a policy possible had disappeared. The networks retained departments of Standards and Practices with individual codes and guidelines still in force, but the power of veto would no longer have the mantle of industry authority.

Family viewing is now little more than a promotional slogan, although certain members of Congress from time to time push for its resurrection.[4] The call to "do something about television" erupts whenever actual violence prompts a public reaction to television or other entertainment media.

Moderation, restraint, codes, broadcaster responsibility—all these terms appear in the national dialogue in times of crisis. If the Family Viewing Policy failed to work—and it was, in my opinion, unworkable—then what vehicle could suffice today? The creative community, if anything, is more unfettered, with more venues for programming. Broadcasters are under more competitive pressures. Our society remains obsessed with guns and violence. Only the need for a scapegoat remains. Perhaps public pressure will again produce a vehicle to dampen or mitigate the flow of violence in entertainment. Time will tell.

A Television Ratings System

An industry-created system now provides ratings and some labeling on some television programs on some channels. Whether the ratings will be found constitutional in the courts remains uncertain, but, from my perspective, a different labeling system would have been preferable and more useful to viewers, although I continue to question the usefulness of ratings for television. The television industry had to act in the face of renewed government and public pressure, but it seems to me the action occurred without sufficient attention to existing standards procedures.

On December 18, 1996, the television industry unveiled the following six-category, age-based ratings system. TV-Y indicates suitability for all children. TV-Y7 is programming directed to children over age seven. G is for the general audience, all ages. TV-PG designates a program that contains material parents might find unsuitable for younger children. A TV-14 rating cautions parents of material unsuitable for children under fourteen, and TV-M or MA indicates a program specifically designed for adults and might not be suitable for children under seventeen. Beginning January 1, 1997, the rating appeared for fifteen seconds in the upper left-hand corner of the screen—if the broadcaster or cable operator had agreed to participate in the effort.

The industry, or rather some segments of the industry, created the ratings in the wake of the far-reaching 1996 Telecommunications Act. Congress passed the legislation because of concerns about trends in television programming fostered by the extremely competitive environment and technological developments that might increase the programming experimentation to retain an audience. That act contained two provisions that pushed development of a ratings system.

With the FCC and manufacturers left to decide when, the legislation required television sets manufactured sometime after 1998 to be equipped with a V-chip, a device to enable a viewer to block display of all programs with a common rating. The second provision stated that the FCC, with advice from an advisory committee, could prescribe a ratings system for television programs containing "sexual, violent or other indecent material about which parents should be informed before it is displayed to children." The act, however, stayed the effectiveness of this provision for one year to enable the industry itself to establish a "voluntary" rating system.

After a series of debates over questions of censorship, which system to adopt, who would designate the ratings, and whether news programs would be included, the previously described age-based system was accepted by the broadcasters and cable operators as the least onerous form of capitulation to politicians and pressure groups.

Some six months later, after threats of further congressional action, the system was modified to "better identify programs containing sex, violence, adult themes and offensive language."[1] Under the revised system, programs rated TV-PG, TV-14, or TV-M would be further designated with labels: S for sex, V for violence, L for crude language, and D for dialogue containing sexual themes.[2] The letter would appear alongside the age-based rating in the upper left-hand corner of the screen. Also an FV, for fantasy violence, designation would be added to the TV-Y7 category for cartoons or fantasy programs aimed at older children.

Five individuals, most of them parents, would join the broadcasters/cable operators/creative industry panel Review Board. In exchange for this, Congress agreed in July 1997 to hold off for at least three years any further legislation in this matter.[3] ABC, CBS, Fox, and most cable networks went along with the new arrangement, but NBC and some small cable channels declined to participate. NBC retained an age-based system with additional advisories at the network's discretion. NBC released a statement that its leadership saw no place for government involvement in what is seen on television, which fell short of a court challenge.

When first proposed in 1996, I was opposed to the establishment of a ratings system, but recognized the practical reality that some action was required. A potent coalition—the president of the United States, a conservative Congress, the PTA, and some academics—united to call for a ratings system.

Different groups had different plans, and the climate was not one in which principle or constitutional arguments could prevail. It was a climate in which I saw the networks and cable executives caving to political pressure and a piece of legislation that as the Family Viewing experience bore witness, could be costly, drawn out, and wasteful in the long run. I recognized as a former combatant that opposition was futile, and I formulated my own compromise solution.

"If We Must Rate TV, Let's Get It Right" was the title of my essay, published in the March 4, 1996, issue of *Broadcasting & Cable*. In that article, I suggested a labeling system supported by advisory information to provide context, because I believed a ratings system based on the classifications used for theatrical movies would be a mistake. My disagreements with Dr. Richard Heffner, then chairman of the Rating and Classification Administration of the MPAA, were detailed in chapter 4. In theory, the MPAA's system does more than advise; it serves as a gatekeeper. An R rating requires those under seventeen entering a theater to be accompanied by a parent or adult guardian. Yet, in 1999, we were still debating how best to implement this provision. Theater owners have agreed to require ID for purchase of a ticket, but critics have pointed out the many ways a teenager can circumvent the requirement.

A television rating carries an even more reduced possibility of usefulness. The latchkey child, the child watching his own set, or a child whose parents or caretaker do not exert responsibility for viewing makes his own decision. The warning system also provides the illusion of protection, because it can become a surrogate for responsible parental supervision, discussion, and watching together. In the thirty years I supervised the editing of theatrical motion pictures, I can recall only one film that was originally rated R that was not edited to the equivalent of a PG or at least PG-13.

I also believed an age-based system that provided no context information would be too ambiguous for responsible parents to use in selecting programs for a child's viewing. I had learned from my experiences which types of advisories worked and which did not. As the person responsible for designing an advisory system that brought the statement "Tonight's episode deals with 'mature subject matter' " into the television world, I knew that a system that simply attaches an R, a PG-13 or an equally ambiguous symbol to television programs for fifteen seconds would do nothing constructive to alleviate the problem.

In the early 1970s, ABC first began to use "advisories" to alert parents to content of programs that might be unsuitable for younger children. This action was in response to congressional hearings and public concern about the effect of violent portrayals in television programs on the behavior of children. We began by adding an advisory to certain episodes of *Baretta*, a high-action detective drama starring Robert Blake. We used the following language in audio and video: "Tonight's episode of 'Baretta' deals with mature subject matter. Parental judgment and discretion advised." A shorter version was used on all on-air promotions and in newspaper listings.

While visiting a communications class at the University of Georgia, I heard the assertion by a professor of sociology, based on a study he had conducted, that the phrase "mature subject matter" provided no real information. After a prolonged seminar debate, I was convinced that if our intent was to inform, we needed to do more. After that discussion, ABC used additional language to describe content more specifically.

For example, the theatrical motion picture *Taxi Driver*, edited for television before telecast, carried this warning: "The following film, edited for television, contains graphic depictions of violence. Parental discretion is advised." In addition, an end crawl stated: "In the aftermath of violence, the distinction between hero and villain is sometimes a matter of interpretation or misinterpretation of facts. 'Taxi Driver' suggests that tragic error can be made. The Filmmakers."

The inclusion of the end crawl illustrates the point of applying standards that take into consideration factors other than the acts of violence themselves. Not only was a "warning" appropriate in this case, but the film's ending dictated a caveat relevant to the final impression on the viewer. This example illustrates advantages of an advisory system over a ratings system if the true objective is to transmit information to the parent or any viewer.

If television were going to play the "ratings game," the approach needed to focus on labeling, not rating, programs to provide enough context and additional information to allow parents to make a judgment about the appropriateness of the program. Although the debate centered on the impact of violence portrayals on children, it should be noted that viewers of all ages can be offended or disturbed by excessive or gratuitous depictions of violence.

My experience also made me aware of the complicated nature of censorship in the creative process. To maintain the viability of the medium, the creative community needs the tools of effective storytelling, drama, passion, and conflict, and, in some cases, realistic depiction of violence.

A labeling system must also be simple enough that the creative nuances of some three-thousand hours of prime-time programming do not involve the raters in hairsplitting decisions. Time is another factor, because frequently, the final print is not ready until hours before air. I suggested the following: MA—MILD ACTION, A—ACTION, S—SEX, L—LANGUAGE, and F—FAMILY. The letter, which would convey the essential quality, would appear not only at the beginning of the program, but also in on-air promotions and newspaper and magazine ads and listings. In addition, an "advisory" would be used where appropriate to provide additional information about the context.

Whether or not the industry took note of my recommendations, the first effort was the age-based ratings system, described earlier, and the expansion, under pressure, into letter labels and continued use of advisories.

The calls to "clean up television" continue despite the ratings systems. In the May 31, 1999, issue of *Broadcasting & Cable*, an article entitled "Senator Targets Broadcast Licenses" reports that "lawmakers . . . call on TV to clean up its content, saying programmers are using the newly developed TV ratings system as an excuse to put even more objectionable content on TV."

In the fall of 1999, a group of legislators wrote to the heads of the six networks, urging the reinstatement of the Family Viewing Hour, because the lawmakers claimed studies showed 1999 prime-time programs contained "more violence, profanity and sexual depictions than ever."

Clearly, such concerns are not without merit, which leads me to my primary reason, in principle, to oppose a ratings system. First however useful a rating system may be in aiding parents in choosing the appropriate fare for children, it is no substitute for prior script review and the application of guidelines to entertainment programming. Standards that require depictions of violence to be reasonably related to plot development or character delineation go to the essence of the broadcasting industry's responsibility to act in the public interest. The avoidance of sensationalism and exploitation in sexual depictions is often a matter of degree in camera angles and innuendos, which can be controlled by an editor's careful review of script and tape or film.

It is not well known outside the television industry that the television networks have Standards and Practices departments. These editors/censors, charged with the responsibility to oversee programming content, operate independently of the program or sales departments, as I have previously described. The function of the Standards and Practices department is to restrict "excessive" and "gratuitous" violence and eliminate the "sensational and exploitative" in television programs.

If the censors do their job properly, there is no need for a ratings system, because no R program would ever air. This was certainly true during my employment at ABC, but I am uncertain whether the same statement can be made today, although it should be the case if the editor continues to operate in the same fashion.

Obviously, the television set does not have the theater manager at the door asking the viewer if he/she is thirteen or seventeen or older. Even if certain scenes were borderline, a warning or disclaimer both on the program and in the promotional material and in newspaper and *TV Guide* ads would alert the parent. If there is a failure or error in judgment made in the review process, then, of course, there would be critical retribution or advertiser rejection.

Self-regulation is more efficient in a democratic society than government-imposed rules. The function of internal censorship in television serves as an effective compromise between the demands of the creative community for freedom of expression and the broadcasters' public-interest responsibility. Unlike the ratings system that assigns a classification, this procedure is much more subjective and nuanced. Standards are guidelines for subjective judgments in selection, interpretation, and direction. Does it work? Not all the time. Not everyone agrees with a perception or an outcome. Errors are made and what may appear acceptable on paper may turn out excessive on the screen. The point is, however, that this system when operated in good faith gives more control over the program than a mere label. In my view, standards review succeeded most of the time.

I am troubled by creation of a ratings system that assumes the failure of content review, which has operated for many years in the television industry. Why should a technological device, the V-chip, make editorial judgment obsolete? The availability of a mechanical device should not dictate an impractical solution to a problem for which there exists a working, if not perfect, remedy. If—and that's a big if—the industry were able to cast political considerations aside, the current procedure to deal with the portrayal of violence and sex on television would be more effective than any ratings system. The retention of this structure is essential to the objective of informing the public as to program content. To destroy it is to lose the sophisticated human interface process between the writer/producer and the responsible broadcaster in the creation of acceptable viewing for America's television audience.

A final word. As long as our society fosters the conditions that create violence, crime or antisocial behavior, violent depictions, whether in news coverage or dramatic portrayal, will be with us. As long as good storytelling relies on conflict, as by definition it does, crimes of passion, whodunits, horror, and jeopardy will be intrinsic to drama. To scapegoat the messenger for the ills of society or to stifle creative efforts to shock, create suspense, frighten, enlighten, and entertain the audience will not diminish the problem. The task of managers, programmers, creators, and editors is to exercise a standard of reasonableness. The amount and frequency of such material is within the control of the broadcaster or cable operator. The quality and depth of character portrayal and plot development is within the control of the writer/producer. What is excessive or gratuitous changes with the storytelling. Context, consequences, humor, direction, and performance all determine how much is too much.

Such an approach requires a definitive commitment, a commitment to continuity, consistency, and conscience, by the broadcaster, and a commitment to exercise responsibility by the parent. The parent must know his child—what he can absorb, what he can be permitted to watch, and how much. The broadcaster must set the limits and guidelines, guidelines that provide some flexibility for innovation and experimentation and respect creative freedom with a sense of accountability. Warnings, ratings, and disclosures are merely devices to prepare an audience. They are after-the-fact information, sometimes useful, but never a substitute for editorial judgment about the content or industry responsibility for programming.

Speaking the Truth

Preserving the Integrity of the Docudrama

In recent years, it has become increasingly difficult to separate fact from fiction, not only in television docudramas, but also in all forms of creative endeavors from novels to movies, even in some areas of journalism.[1] Reenactments of events with some of the real participants on television news magazines is disturbing and dangerous. Dramatic license, in my view, has far exceeded its boundaries, and the most egregious recent example is Edmund Morris's biography of President Ronald Reagan. What is more distressing and, I believe, dangerous to the flow of information is the frequency and the casualness of this blending of facts and fiction in all media.

In the October 1992 special issue of *American Heritage,* in "Power of the Historical Novel," Daniel Aaron paraphrases the columnist George Will by stating, "If novelists use 'the raw material of history—real people, important events,' then they should be constrained by concern for truthfulness, by respect for the record and a judicious weighing of possibilities."[2]

This chapter deals with "truth" as it relates to production of the television docudrama. Truth is essential to this entertainment genre, especially because of its proximity to hard news. Truth is a complex concept. There are facts that may be in dispute and points of view that must be weighted to discover the essence of truth. Over the years, in television and in motion pictures, the docudrama has been criticized by reviewers and academicians for distortion, for tampering with "truth."

The number of docudramas is on the increase. The genre, which dramatizes real events about real people, requires limited dramatic license, but the amount and scope of the license is the sticking point. The difficulty arises when fact and fiction are mixed, when for dramatic purposes, a fact is blurred or embellished. Another aspect is the selection of the facts that enhance the author's point of view. Even though docudrama often treats relatively recent events, within the past two or three decades, many younger Americans have learned of an event first from a television docudrama. What criteria are needed to preserve the integrity of the facts within the context of the drama?

A good place to begin an examination of the docudrama form is the motion picture *JFK,* written, directed, and produced by Oliver Stone, who gave his interpretation to the events surrounding the assassination of President John F. Kennedy. The outcry against Stone's "distortion" of the facts was loud and vociferous. In his defense, he appeared to say that as an author he is allowed to hypothesize and is not required to use facts with substance, but to draw his own conclusions.

In my view, that approach should be labeled personal opinion; it is not docudrama. Based on my legal background, my attitude has always been that conclusions must be based on facts, although limited dramatic license is permissible and some incidental fictionalization. Advocacy is prohibited. Conflicting points of view must be presented.

In 1979, writers, producers, directors, and broadcasters came together in Ojai, California, to talk about the genre, which then appeared to be in danger. The consensus at that important gathering, and time has borne it out, was that the docudrama is a viable program technique. Reduced to its simplest form, docudrama is no more or less than the relating of a story, based on real events and real people. The story has to entertain and captivate to be a commercial success. The difficulty arises when an author interprets the fact or creates "fact" to sustain his point of view, which is presented as undeniable truth. When the narrative takes on the emotional and intellectual flavor of the writer, the story takes yet another step away from the "truth." This brings us to the roots of the controversy: (1) what is fact and what is fiction? and (2) where is the line between exposition and advocacy? If it is "fiction," it is not "truth." If it is not truth, it is not "docudrama." By definition, then, for television and, in my view, for motion pictures as well, a standard of fidelity is required.

David Rintels, television writer, dramatist, and scholar, summed up the challenge at that Ojai meeting. He said, "The public interest demands the best efforts of all of us to save this vital source of information and drama."

It is critical for television writers/producers to separate questions of substance from questions of procedure. If docudrama is the telling of "history," then in the telling, current thinking and perspective on controversial issues are affected. Guidelines about what is or is not permissible in dealing with perceived fact as distinguished from invented happenings must be used to ensure fair and accurate treatment of the issues.

Why should television docudramas come in for special care? Because of the nature of the medium. Television often presents entertainment and news events in proximity, which means a higher degree of care is required. First, there is the ever present potential that a teleplay will be interrupted for a news bulletin or special news report. Reality and fantasy may be juxtaposed. This has the potential of confusing the viewer. Is it news, which is presumed true, or is it drama based on news, which, it follows, must also be true?

Second, the viewer may receive his only recounting or interpretation of an event from television. This possibility makes it imperative for the broadcaster to ensure that clear distinctions be made between what is fact, what is opinion, what is fiction. If a docudrama mixes the three ingredients without adequate safeguards and/or disclosure, is not the viewer misled?

Viewing a television docudrama is different from selecting a book from among a variety of resources in the library. It also differs from exposure to the many different points of view in a print debate of a motion picture such as *JFK*. In television docudrama, there is one narrative, perhaps a brief review of the plot in a television guide, and, except for whatever idea or impression made on the viewer, it is then gone forever.

The potential size of the audience—the actual audience that derives information, ideas, or values from its message—is a factor. It demands a degree of caution that suggests fairness in the presentation of conflicting points of view to allow the viewer to come to his own conclusions.

The inherent limits on a viewer's choices in television require that more than one side of a controversial issue must be explored. Choice is not available unless the viewer is shown conflicting facts and opposing views. To achieve the goal, choice, the docudrama must meet certain criteria. To explore controversial issues, it must present more than one side. The author's interpretation of fact or the historian's deductions or inferences must be made clear in a docudrama presentation. Fabrication of an event, resequencing of time and happenings, or invention of totally fictitious characters, which are passed off as truth, invalidates the presentation as docudrama.

Edward Jay Epstein, the scholarly author who participated in a town hall panel debate on the movie *JFK*, made the distinction between fiction and nonfiction as follows: "In non-fiction the writer is bound by the universe of discoverable fact when he reaches the limits of discoverable fact, he stops. . . . The problem comes when an artist tries to mix fact and fiction. What you get is not a hybrid but pure fiction, because the introduction of a fictional scene or fact changes everything after it."[3] That is substantive criteria.

Certain procedures provide guidance for an author who wants to avoid the pitfalls. David Rintels in a *New York Times* article states:

> Most writers who dramatize real people and events have a moral code that tells them:
>
> Make no changes that are not absolutely necessary to tell the story better, more understandably.
>
> Make no change in the facts when the facts are not in dispute or subject to misinterpretation.
>
> Never change the essence of the story or the event, or the character.
>
> Make no change that will make a difference as to how history is perceived.
>
> Make no change when a participant in the event will be unfairly damaged.
>
> Never invent unless it is necessary to fill a gap, or for reasons of completeness or clarity. Never invent *at all unless* you believe the invention will illuminate and not distort reality.

To that most critical issue, invention, I would add that there should be a reasonable basis in circumstance or surrounding events for the "invention."

Here are some of the criteria we developed at ABC for the docudrama:

> It is permissible to create composite characters (i.e., characters who are based on two or more actual individuals). However, fictitious characters—other than incidental characters who have little or no bearing on the basic plot—should not be included.
>
> The chronology of significant actual events portrayed should be substantially accurate, and supportive evidence produced. Telescoping may be employed so long as the compression does not misrepresent actual events. Where relevant to accuracy, passages of time must be clearly indicated, either in dialogue, by super, dissolves, or other visual techniques.
>
> Personal characteristics, attitudes and the demeanor of actual persons portrayed must be consistent with corroborating evidence as to the actual characteristics of these persons.
>
> Created dialogue must be consistent with the actions, values, attitudes and personalities of the actual figures portrayed.
>
> Fictionalized or compressed representations of actual events must be reasonably consistent with the historical record regarding them. For example; although a conversation between actual persons on a specific matter may not be capable of documentation, depictions of such conversation may be acceptable if they accurately characterize the individuals portrayed and their specific attitudes at the time in which the scene is de-

picted and if they are consistent with available evidence regarding their action and thoughts—i.e., no invention out of whole cloth.

Implementation of such guidelines is, of course, subjective, but inter-pretation of facts, selection of events, and perception of persona are all judg-ments, a mixture of the heart and mind. History is the handmaiden of the writer's selection process. The reasonable-care standard and the best rule of evidence govern the acceptability of inclusion or exclusion of material. Good faith representation, fairness, and reliable sources are prerequisites.

For example, in the prayer scene in the television adaptation of Wood-ward and Bernstein's *The Final Days*, Richard Nixon is portrayed as dis-traught and stricken in an emotion-filled meeting to which he had invited Henry Kissinger. We sought substantiation and documentation for this scene.

Several different accounts exist in print. The television producers in-tended to follow their version of the meeting[4] that included Nixon break-ing down and sobbing. Also contained in the same scene was his request, as quoted in the book, "Henry, please don't ever tell anyone that I cried and that I was not strong."

In the Woodward/Bernstein book, the statement is not made during their meeting in the Lincoln Room, but in a subsequent telephone call from Nixon to Kissinger, after Kissinger's return to his office, where two col-leagues are present.

The authors' corroboration for the statement is Kissinger's custom of having a colleague listen in on an extension to his conversation with Nixon. The book relates the conversation but makes no attribution to Kissinger or a colleague regarding the quote. In Kissinger's rendition of the meeting and telephone call in his autobiography *Years of Upheaval*,[5] he refers to the prayer scene. Kissinger states he is not clear as to whether he knelt, which he calls a "trivial distinction." He refers to Nixon as being "shattered," "deeply distraught," "stricken," but states that he was not out of control although " I found his visible agony more natural than the al-most inhuman self containment that I had known so well." He refers to the telephone call, but says nothing about anyone listening on an extension. He states that Nixon asked that "I must not remember our encounter that evening as a sign of weakness," and that "he hoped that I would keep in mind the times when he had been strong." Kissinger goes on to state that Nixon asked him that if and when he spoke of the evening, he did so with respect. Kissinger made no reference to Nixon's sobbing.

Richard Nixon, in his memoirs, refers to having prayed with Kissinger that evening but does not indicate that he broke down and sobbed. Woodward attested to the accuracy of the version based on their book. The television version had to take into account several different sets of facts, perceptions of "fact," emotion, and interpretation. Care was used in its portrayal, and telescoping of events was permitted to attempt to reach a consensus of attitude, representation, and circumstance of the event.

Another example involves the depiction of chronology in *Attica*, a teleplay based on Tom Wicker's book, *A Time to Die*. A question arose about the actual sequence of events. In the first script, the order to storm the yard, where the prisoners held guards hostage, came before prisoners brought out some hostages and held knives to their throats. Was this act a bluff by the prisoners, as some believed, or a threat to harm hostages, which caused corrections Commissioner Russell Oswald to give the order to proceed? To accept the scripted version was to conclude action without cause. To reject the script version was to justify the order. After review of the literature, the McKay report, which investigated the uprising, Tom Wicker's description of the event in his book, and *Time* reports and articles about the event, ABC Broadcast Standards and Practices requested a reversal of the sequence. This meant the teleplay suggested some cause for the attack instead of an accusation about which there was some ambiguity. The weight-of-the-evidence rule governed in this case.

Sometimes only a disclosure statement suffices to explain the dramatization of dialogue and scenes. In *Separate but Equal,* a dramatization of *Brown vs. Board of Education,* a key debate takes place at Howard University. Educators, lawyers, and students discuss the merits of taking the case to the Supreme Court. Should they risk a negative decision? How will the court rule on constitutional rights and states' rights? Are equal facilities preferable to integration? Thurgood Marshall's position to proceed to the highest court of the land is firm. Not knowing exactly what Marshall said, the script creates certain dialogue and includes in Marshall's decisive remarks eloquent paraphrases of thoughts voiced by James Nabrit, a Howard law professor.

Harry Briggs Jr. is a representative black school child and composite character. Mrs. Briggs says her son didn't walk miles to school, only a couple of blocks from home to school, but many other students did. In another example of distortion, John W. Davis, the attorney who represents South Carolina in *Brown vs. Board of Education* before the Supreme Court, is purported to have won the famous steel case *Youngstown Sheet and Tube vs. Sawyer* in the Supreme Court before he accepts Governor Byrnes's offer to represent South Carolina. Davis, in fact, did not win the steel case before he accepted Byrnes's offer, but he did argue the steel case before he argued Brown. With this background, ABC ran this disclosure: "Tonight's film is a dramatization based on interviews and accounts of the time, and contains created scenes and dialogue."

The most delicate question in the docudrama debate is that of "point of view." The bottom line in creation of a story canvas that offers the viewer choices is to handle truth responsibly in terms of accuracy. Certainly, fact is as perceived in the eye of the beholder. Truth is subject to translation both in word and in picture. But, as previously stated, the teleplay limits the viewer's access to information to that one visual volume. The tremendous impact of that one visual story, not only on the adult viewer, but also on a child's perception of history, places a heavy mantle on the shoulder of the broadcaster and author. Consider the impact on a young audience who remembers neither Presidents Lyndon Johnson or John F. Kennedy of the television airing of *JFK,* which alleges Johnson's complicity in Kennedy's assassination.

Many writers take issue with this concern for balance; they argue the writer is entitled to a point of view and cannot write well without a single perspective. Responsibility, they claim, should not make for blandness nor does balance ensure fairness and honesty. Obviously, the closer the subject to the present time the more likely the difficulty and controversy of speaking the truth.

I don't believe the problem is without solution. One obvious but not totally satisfactory answer is disclosure. I have often said that there is nothing wrong with putting a rigged quiz show on the air if you disclose at the beginning, middle, or end, "This show is rigged." Not the answer, but one step to balance the interests in pursuit of the goal.

Another suggestion is to follow the television program with a panel discussion or present another full program with the opposing point of view. The latter perhaps is not as commercially feasible as the former, but doable. The proliferation of distribution systems, including cable, satellite, and additional networks, makes this possible. Why not include a bibliography at the end of the program and, where appropriate, publish a teacher's guide to supplement and clarify the production?

Surely, fertile minds writing for this industry and those critiquing its content can achieve a consensus of standard procedure to enable this viable form to continue to entertain, inform, and enlighten. That is the easy part, the more difficult one is for all to accept the substantive requirements of accuracy, fairness, balance, and choice.

As a footnote to this discussion of the docudrama and the concept of balance, I think it appropriate to comment on the passing of the Fairness Doctrine. Until it was repealed in 1987, this FCC administrative policy served as a guidepost for insuring fairness and balance in television presentations. The Fairness Doctrine had its roots in the FCC's 1949 *Report on Editorializing by Broadcast Licensees.* The regulatory intent was political in that the commission, supported by Congress, wanted to insure fairness in the political arena. Although it did not require "equal time" for candidates, which was provided in section 315 of the Communications Act of 1934, it did set forth the affirmative obligation upon broadcasters to afford reasonable opportunity for the discussion of conflicting views on issues of public importance.

The Fairness Doctrine as it existed for almost three decades imposed two essential affirmative responsibilities on broadcasters: adequate coverage of issues of public importance and that the treatment must fairly reflect differing viewpoints. The second responsibility was most important to our standards process, because it related to questions of balance and "point of view" in the docudrama.

In 1969, the Supreme Court addressed the constitutionality of the doctrine in the Red Lion case.[6] The Court rejected the broadcasters' First Amendment challenge to the Fairness Doctrine and related rules governing personal attack and political editorials. The Court justified limits on the First Amendment protection of broadcasting based upon the doctrine of "scarcity." Given the limited number of broadcast frequencies, the Court reasoned that "only a tiny fraction of those with resources and intelligence can hope to communicate by radio at the same time . . . even if the entire spectrum is utilized in the present state of commercially acceptable technology" (395 U.S. at 388).[7] Although challenged many times since 1969, the "scarcity" doctrine has survived in Supreme Court decisions relating to broadcasting matters.

In the 1980s, in the middle of deregulation fever, the FCC disagreed with the philosophy of scarcity and believed that because of the proliferation of cable and satellite broadcasting and the increasing diversity of distribution, the Fairness Doctrine was no longer necessary.

I mourn the demise of the Fairness Doctrine. For many years it served as a standard, both in spirit and in law, that enabled us to implement our policy of "exposition, not advocacy." The doctrine reinforced the BS&P argument that television should offer the viewer a choice of viewpoints, not solely that of the producer. In my view, television was to teach, not preach, and with an obligation to provide information not propaganda. Over the years, the Supreme Court has held that the "public's right to know" is not to be interpreted as a right of access.

The doctrine made good public policy; it made for good business policy. It helped us ensure the public would be given information to enable it to make reasoned decisions based on full disclosure, a fair and representative or balanced presentation of all sides of a controversy. Compliance with such a policy is no more or less than an extension of the licensee's obligation to operate "in the public interest."

With journalistic standards, program formats, and content selection today more often than not dictated by the competitive marketplace created by the pressures of multiple distribution systems, the need is all the more paramount for guidelines defining public-interest requirements for those entrusted with a public asset. In an industry that is exploding and obliterating standards in the process, it behooves policy makers and responsible broadcasters to establish guidelines for the fair and responsible conduct of those who have the means to keep the public informed.

Censorship and the Censor's Role

This book has described the form of censorship I practiced at ABC television for thirty years. I use the word "form," because my activities were not limited to the blue pencil or the editor's scissors, the restriction and deletion of material, but involved decisions more akin to editor than censor. Whether I was an editor or a censor depends upon your perspective, and I am certain that there are those who would take strong exception to my definition. Whatever the definition, the work I did and the responsibility I exercised may soon disappear.

Diversity of distribution systems, television on the Internet, the advent of the V-chip to supplement the new ratings system, the maturation or indifference of the audience, and the digitization of the broadcasting signal contribute to a vast wave of change that is sweeping over the communications business.

From a legal and practical standpoint, how do you censor the Internet? Providers and search engines are nothing more than common carriers, and only limited technological controls are available to police the Internet. The First Amendment does not apply internationally, and with millions of Web sites already on-line, it's impractical to apply editorial standards to existing or future web sites.

With more than a hundred channels potentially available in the home, isn't it up to the parent to decide what a child watches? Or is even the idea of parental supervision antiquated? The audience today is more receptive to material that would have been found offensive in the past. Matters of sexuality certainly bother people less and disturb more infrequently. Although concerns remain about the quality of programs for children and the extent to which violent material induces violent behavior, the management of such material becomes an impossible task as programming sources proliferate.

Perhaps, in a democracy, the demise of programming censorship is as it should be. The balancing function merges with the principle of freedom of choice, and the viewer has the prime responsibility to make the ultimate decision.

The First Amendment protects free speech against governmental action and, in most cases, from prior restraints. In the two centuries since adoption of the Bill of Rights, the boundaries of free speech, politically and personally, have been defined in various ways with the impetus always toward the free flow of ideas and information.

When the Communications Acts of 1927, 1934, and 1996 were written, Congress each time incorporated the principle of free speech in the "no censorship" provision[1] of the acts. At the same time, Congress set a standard for the granting of a license to operate a radio or television station. That standard, vague and ambiguous as it may be, requires that an owner of a license must operate "in the public interest." The act states: "The Commission (FCC), if public convenience, interest, or necessity will be served thereby . . . shall grant . . . a station license."[2] The "public interest" standard defines a station operator's service requirement.

Although the requirements of compliance have been eviscerated over the past several years, the mandate still contains "public interest," which, at the very least, requires the exercise of due care where children are concerned. This amorphous concept of "public interest" retains some sense of respect for family and order in society and support for institutional values. Perhaps one can go even further. Application and interpretation of such terms as fairness, balance, truth, and dignity of the human spirit can also be attributed to its meaning.

When I began, a censor needed to understand the interrelationship of the historic force of free speech and public interest plus the business structure of the industry. Broadcasting in the United States operates in a free enterprise system, answerable to shareholders or private entrepreneurs, to produce a profit. A network is a voluntary affiliation of stations, each station in a contractual relationship with the network. The stations, in essence, buy programs, produced by the network or licensed by the network from others, which each could not afford to produce individually. In exchange, the stations grant the network time to sell advertisements within or adjacent to the programs.

The business structure of commercial broadcasting means programs must be scheduled that appeal to the most viewers. The underlying question in every programming decision: will the audience tune in? The second question: will the affiliates air this program? And the critical third question: will the advertisers buy time?

In a sense, programming decisions based on these three economic forces are all censorial activities not unlike the function of those of us who act as editors/censors in the review of program content for questions of taste, acceptability, language, violent portrayals, and sexual innuendos. In legal fact, the First Amendment does not apply to activities of a private individual or corporation. The amendment's prohibition is against congressional or governmental action. Editorial review, deletion, revision of material, whether for print or broadcast, does not violate the First Amendment.

In chapter 9, which deals with the Family Viewing Hour, we saw that a lower federal court held that coercion by the chairman of the FCC and acquiescence by the National Association of Broadcasters and the three national networks constituted government action. The decision was vacated for procedural reasons by an appellate court and was never really decided by the courts, although the FCC found no such conspiracy that could be deemed government action.

In the world of ideas and creativity, the concept of freedom of speech is so ingrained in the American psyche that it pervades television in spirit if not in law. Television is also unique in that it transmits news and information programs on the same channel with entertainment programs.

Until the recent technological advances, television has been differentiated from print media by the scarcity principle—not enough space or time for all the people who want to be heard. The Supreme Court recognized this reality in its decision in the Red Lion case.[3] In considering FCC action in connection with the application of the Fairness Doctrine, which is now defunct, it applied the "rational basis" criteria to broadcasting issues balancing public interest and free speech considerations.

In our system several themes govern the definitions of the censor's role. (1)The government cannot censor except where there is a finding that there is an important governmental interest at stake—a public-interest obligation—that outweighs a freedom of speech privilege. (2) An individual or private corporation can censor as long as its action is not conspiratorial nor collaborative with government action and is not discriminatory. (3) The spirit of the law recognizes freedom of expression as a concomitant of creativity in a democratic society. (4) At the foundation is the democratic concept that freedom of choice is the people's right.

What, then, is "the public interest"? In all the legislation relating to broadcasting or communications, "public interest, convenience and necessity" are never defined. The legislative history is of little help nor do court decisions provide much guidance about compliance standards. The terms have generally been defined case by case.

At one time FCC rules and regulations and some FCC decisions drew a road map; in the 1940s and 1950s some FCC actions even dealt with program matters. Prohibition of obscenity, horse racing regulations, lottery restrictions, excessive suspense on children's programs, false or fraudulent advertising, and other like program practices[4] defined station accountability at license renewal time. The Fairness Doctrine, until its repeal in 1987, imposed a specific obligation when stations dealt with controversial issues of public importance.

In the 1960s and 1970s, stations were required to "ascertain" the needs and interests of the community in order to serve the public interest. This ascertainment process led to the scheduling of a number of public affairs and documentary programs on a weekly or monthly basis. When the rules were discontinued in the late 1980s, many of the programs disappeared. In the 1960s and 1970s, license renewals were challenged because of programming practices and lack of affirmative action in employment. Minority and women-ownership issues and occasionally advertising and children's program deficiencies also engendered license challenges. As discussed in chapter 6, children's programming required special attention. Concern with the quality of programs designed primarily for children, as evidenced by the 1990 Children's Act, seems to be the only vestige of this once robust regulatory policy. All of these activities contributed to a definition of the "public interest."

In 1987, with the industry already in the middle of major changes, a landmark decision grew out of a comedic routine about words forbidden on the air. George Carlin, a "satirical humorist," gave a twelve-minute monologue entitled "Filthy Words" before a live audience in a California theater; that performance of "the words you couldn't say on the public, ah, airwaves . . . the infamous Seven Dirty Words" was recorded.

On a Tuesday afternoon at two o'clock, the Pacifica Foundation's FM radio station in New York City, WBAI, played the monologue during a discussion about society's attitude about language. That broadcast ignited the debate about indecent programming on radio and television.[5]

In the Pacifica case the Supreme Court held that the FCC had the power to regulate a broadcast that is indecent, but not obscene, despite the First Amendment prohibition against government action. The reasoning behind the decision is pertinent to this discussion of the role of censorship in television.

In Justice John Paul Stevens concluding paragraphs he stated:

> We have long recognized that each medium of expression presents special First Amendment problems. . . . And of all forms of communica-

tion, it is broadcasting that has received the most limited First Amendment protection. . . . A broadcaster may be deprived of his license and his forum if the Commission decides that such an action would serve "the public interest, convenience, and necessity."

The reasons for these distinctions are complex, but two have relevance in the present case. First, the broadcast media have established a *uniquely pervasive presence* [emphasis mine] in the lives of all Americans. Patently offensive, indecent material presented over the airwaves confronts the citizen, not only in public, but also in the privacy of the home, where the *individual's right to be let alone plainly outweighs the First Amendment rights of the intruder.*(Rowan vs. Post Office, 397 U.S. 728 [1970]) [emphasis mine].

Second, broadcasting is uniquely accessible to children, even those too young to read.

We have not decided that an occasional expletive . . . would justify any sanction. . . . The time of day was emphasized by the Commission. . . . We simply hold that when the Commission finds that a pig has entered the parlor, the exercise of its regulatory power does not depend on proof that the pig is obscene.[6]

A broadcasting license became a very fragile commodity, which could be put in jeopardy depending on how "public interest" requirements would be balanced with free speech. That ruling came later in my tenure as censor, but was part of the evolution in the understanding of censorship.

When I first took on the assigned task to oversee the Department of Standards and Practices, I was discouraged by the prospect. The responsibility to enforce rules, which required script deletions and rejection of themes and story lines, in a highly competitive arena with high stakes and rapidly changing tastes, was a formidable one. It was made even more difficult by working at ABC, emerging from a lackluster third place and striving to compete with its two more experienced rivals. ABC had to rely on innovation, experimentation, exploitation, and a high degree of risk to forge ahead. ABC also primarily served major urban areas where tastes were different from those in rural areas and smaller cities. Because of the lack of television stations in some markets, and only two VHF stations permissible in others, ABC was handicapped by the size of its network and had to find programs that grabbed attention quickly and prominently.

I set forth for myself certain criteria to enable me and my staff to function in this cauldron of law, principle, spirit, and commercial reality. Here is my personal credo and interpretation of "the public interest" under which I operated:

Each presentation should be approached with an awareness and respect for the fact that, in an individualistic democratic society, there may be more than one point of view. Notwithstanding the fact that there may be more than one point of view, the majority point of view governs our affairs. Notwithstanding the fact that the majority view governs, the minority view is entitled to expression. Such expression, of either the majority or minority, be had with due respect for the other. Fairness, the dignity of man, and the right to hold one's belief, are basic precepts.

Fairness and dignity, respect for rights of others, dictate (a) that in matters of religion, the honest devotion to devoutness is personal to the individual and disbelief is expressed with due regard for the right to believe, (b) that in matters controversial, both sides are entitled to a hearing, and (c) that social commentary and political satire are a dialogue, not a diatribe, and that the objects of love can be the subject of humor, recognizing that they are, nonetheless, love objects.

Above all, privacy, authority, morality, and ethics can be questioned, but not abused.

I believed that as "censor" I had to be the "corporate conscience," Which meant I had to be a "good citizen" within the confines of the network's legal and regulatory responsibilities to our shareholders and the public. Administration of standards, once they were defined, would require that BS&P operate independently of those responsible for sales, programming decisions, and bottom-line results, Which meant the chief censor had to report directly to top management to ensure independence and objectivity—answering to the chairman and chief executive officer or, in the early days, his senior aide, the executive vice president of the corporation.

In later years, after management changes, the reporting was changed to the president and chief operating officer of the corporation. This was the relationship until the merger with Capital Cities Inc., when the reporting changed again to the general counsel. Although Stephen Weiswasser, the general counsel, was supportive and understood the role and responsibility of the department, this new line weakened the operating authority of BS&P, because Hollywood responds to status and power. The new line of reporting permitted appeals, which often gave more weight to programming considerations and Hollywood relationships than to pure objective weighing of BS&P standards.

Independence from network and station management was necessary to establish objectivity and enforcement in the difficult review and application of standards.

In the light of my credo and within the framework of regulation, license grants, spirit, and competition, I decided that as gatekeeper I would have to balance these sometimes conflicting interests and goals. We would have to apply standards fairly and objectively and, at the same time, in such a manner as to advance rather than impede creative output. The central objective would be to find a way to say yes instead of no. That did not mean always saying yes—definitely no hell's and damn's and no full frontal nudity, except for the death camp scenes in *War and Remembrance,* as described in chapter 5, and no to guns pointed at the screen or displayed in children's programs. In the development of story lines and comedic and dramatic themes, however, the emphasis would be on how to support the creative effort. "Excess" and "truth" sum up the parameters of what was permissible.

No theme or story concept would be deemed unacceptable on the basis of subject alone. Treatment, character delineation, language, and visual depictions all would factor into the determination. In dealing with violence, showing consequences and the extent of harm and its effect on the victim would be weighed heavily. Defusers, such as humor, and slow motion where appropriately used would also be part of the considerations. In that arena, the key word was excess. Was the portrayal too much for the viewer to digest? Was the violence extensive, overdone, exaggerated, or "excessive"? Was it violence merely for the sake of violence?

Sexual depictions required a different approach. Eliminating, for the moment, the harm of abusive and violent sex, which includes other considerations, the expression of love and lovemaking in various forms is to be applauded, not rejected. Once again, however, the judgment centers on questions about excess and sensationalism. Is the portrayal prurient or merely provocative? Is it lustful or salacious? Is it an invasion of privacy? Is it informative, expressive, or abhorrent and overstating?

These types of considerations went into the approval for the telecast of such programs as *That Certain Summer, The Day After, Something about Amelia,* and the series *The Mod Squad, Soap,* and *Thirtysomething.* The BS&P function was not to make the program happen, which was the function of the programming department, but to review the programs in accordance with the dictates of governmental and business considerations.

The role of censor began to define itself in policing the "excessive and gratuitous." This approach would allow for programs that portrayed violence in a context that was story related and was reasonably depicted. It allowed for programs that were sexually provocative or even crude, such as *Three's Company,* which broke new ground but fell short of being prurient or salacious.

Defining "excessive" and "gratuitous" and "sensational" was, of course, difficult, imprecise, and messy. We dealt with subjective meanings, decisions, looking into the eye of the beholder, emotional takeouts, expectations, and impressions. How will the scene be perceived or interpreted? What is the measure of its shock value? For example, the whipping of Kunte Kinte in *Roots* was accepted after watching reactions of those in the story who witnessed the act. The expressions on their faces told us of the hurt and humiliation and brutality conveyed. Consequences were depicted.

Delineating the sensational was just as difficult a process. Was Billie Crystal stereotyping or proselytizing the characteristics of a homosexual? How do you bring the subject of incest to television for the first time? Dare you show nudity in the concentration camp scenes in *War and Remembrance*?

Censoring involved the art of negotiation and compromise. What could stay in, and what had to come out changed with the content, the context, the time period, the depth of cerebral material, the type of costuming, the visual presentation, and whether on- or off-camera, to name just a few factors that influenced decisions over the years. There were rules, but they were subject to interpretation. My job and that of the BS&P staff became a balancing act: of inching ahead or stepping back, of prejudging audience reaction and critical approval, of cautious toe dipping or courageous risk taking.

Sometimes our decisions were applauded, sometimes condemned. But each step taken was with a sense of conscience and a reliance on creative honesty. Experimentation in the spirit of the First Amendment had to be weighed along with accountability to the audience, the stockholder, and the regulator. From the outside looking in, the process was indeed "blue penciling," interfering with the creative process, suppressing ideas. From the inside looking out, the process was balancing interests and rights within the confines of reasonable care and contained permissiveness and a sense of decorum.

An excellent illustration of the issue of decorum centers on the use of language. Early on, the most frequent confrontations resulted from the use of hell's and damn's. Sen. Jesse Helms, before his political career, was a station manager of a successful affiliate in the South. He would call after a screening and scold me for permitting those words to be used. As described in chapter 8, the late Danny Arnold and I almost came to blows over his desire to use the words in a *Barney Miller* episode.

I tried to maintain a sense of civility with respect to the nonoffensive use of language, although crucial decisions did permit inroads from time to time. Such an exception occurred in 1972, when BS&P first screened the theatrical motion picture *Patton* for television. I had no choice but to concede the general's use of "bastards" and "son of a bitch" in two famous scenes, one when he addressed the troops in the opening, the other when he berates a poor frightened soldier for cowardice. ABC placed an audio-video statement at the beginning of the picture, which read in part "ABC reminds viewers that *explicit language* (emphasis mine) is part of this story and urges parental discretion in judging its suitability for younger members of the audience."

The most contentious battles over language did not occur until Stephen Bochco began producing programs for ABC. After the very successful run of his groundbreaking series *Hill Street Blues* on NBC, where he fought major battles with my counterparts in Standards and Practices over questions of sex and language, he developed *Doogie Howser, M.D.*, which ran from 1989 to 1993, and *Cop Rock* in 1990 for the ABC television network.

Cop Rock was a short-lived, innovative dramatic series. The part cop/detective, part musical had cops in a musical dance after chasing down a criminal. Bochco was intent on "rattling people's cages," including ours. In a *USA Today* column by Matt Roush, February 15, 1990, concerning a meeting with me and my L.A. staff, Bochco is quoted as saying: "They're all over me, Geez Louise, you're presiding over the ruination of a medium. I don't want to be reasonable about this. . . . Somebody has to take them on." Then he indirectly attributed audience loss and boredom to our restraints: "We ought to be rattling people's cages."

What brought on these comments was a BS&P request for retribution in a scene where a police officer kills a man and another where the mayor takes a bribe and apparently gets away with it. We drew swords over the use of the word *scumbag,* which I felt was an offensive vulgarity, but Bochco believed appropriate for the situation. It was 1990, after a change in my reporting relationship, and upon management appeal, I lost.

That incident only foreshadowed a more hostile incident about one year later when Bochco used the word *nooky* in a *Doogie Howser, M.D.* script. Doogie Howser was a teenage genius who dealt with problems of growing up, having a girl-friend, and being a licensed physician in residence. Again I felt that the use of the word was crude, offensive, and locker-room slang. It is essentially a sexual term synonymous with "pussy," female genitalia, or coitus. I believed young people, who were the audience for the show, would pick up the term and unwitting of its sexual meaning, misuse the expression.

We went to the dictionaries of Standard English and slang. We went to the English professors at UCLA and elsewhere. We did research on how the word would be perceived. The younger generation either had never heard of the word or did not find it offensive. Their parents and those of my generation knew its meaning and sided with me. It was 1991, and, again on appeal, I lost. So, this anecdote in a way foretells the future and again the change in culture and usage and digestibility of language and actions as we proceed into the twenty-first century.

Another program form where battles are certain in the future is the docudrama. The mixing of fact and fiction has less to do with taste and acceptability than with telling the truth. What was our responsibility in the retelling of events and the role people played in those events in terms of the accuracy of the account? This was not so much a question of censorship as it was a question of reporting the factual correctness or particularity of history.

Stephen Weiswasser, Capital Cities/ABC general counsel, to whom I reported, was a former clerk to the renowned federal appeals court judge David Bazelon and fellow alumni of Harvard Law School. We debated whether "truth" was absolute or relative. Was dramatic license a given or something to be granted stringently? Was "essential truth" an appropriate standard or did we have to hold a producer to a higher mark? Was time a factor in these deliberations? The substance of this discussion was covered in chapter 10 on the docudrama.

The debate is not over, because the trend to mix fact and fiction accelerates in a social and political climate that seems unconcerned about liberties taken with accuracy in historical or current events. I believe we face a serious challenge in keeping our society informed and, therefore, able to make rational and intelligent decisions based on verifiable, substantive, and reliable facts. Democracy surely will wither if distortion, inaccuracy, or invention become the stables upon which decision makers come to rely.

The role of censor clearly changed as television changed. Few rules were written in stone and often an intelligent dialogue brought about revisions that were acceptable to the censor and the creator. Censorship in television was a review process that oversaw the production of entertainment programming and subjected words and pictures to deletion. It was also a creative process that sought to find the path to let it happen. That role soon may be a historical footnote.

As stated in the beginning of this chapter, technological changes, diversity of offerings, and shifts in audience attitudes are contributing to the demise of the self-regulatory standards review process. Is this "good" for society? Is freedom to choose from an abundance of programs a satisfactory substitute for surrogate judgment as to appropriateness in matters of taste, in the degree of violent portrayals, and in the presentation of sexual encounters? Need we have a checker of facts? Who is to hold the line against propaganda and polemic in favor of an objective and fairly balanced presentation?

Can we trust marketplace mentality and creative competitive juices to give diligent consideration to the "public interest"?

Can we trust those in power over the most influential medium yet devised by man for communication of ideas to set aside financial and political considerations when making programming choices?

How important is it to maintain that trust in a society beset with debates over the right to bear arms, the necessity for affirmative action programs, racial understanding, sexual preference, prayer in the schools, public education, not to mention questions of foreign policy?

Is there a need today for a gatekeeper?

My answer, prejudiced perhaps, is a qualified yes based on two concepts: checks and balances that the founding fathers built into the Constitution and recognition that to maintain a civil society certain traffic signs are necessary to prevent crashes. Together, these precepts speak to a reasonable self regulatory system that ensures that public-interest considerations and all the other questions above are dealt with in objectively and fairly. This is especially the case because the license to broadcast is a gift from the people and reaches into more than 250 million homes as an invited guest.

The system of checks and balances should serve as an operational model for the application of reasonable standards to take into account three major concerns of our society. First, because the troubling problems of a violent society exist, we need standards to deal with the degree and amount of violence that can be portrayed on the screen. Second, without a shared platform for divergent attitudes toward sexuality, we need to exercise care with respect to the time, manner, and explicitness of portrayal. Third, we need to maintain a guide to outline the degree of factual accuracy required in telling history.

We must balance the imperatives of free speech and free enterprise. Without some measure of gatekeeping, the forces that control the marketplace and the rewards that adhere to a successful program product will leave us with an incoherent and inchoate culture. On the other hand, a process that is reasonable in its administration and cognizant of change in its deliberations will leave us with a popular culture that we can pass along to generations with confidence as to its dignity, fairness, integrity, and inspiration.

NOTES

INDEX

Notes

Overview

1. *Columbia Broadcasting System, Inc. v. Democratic National Committee,* 412 U.S. 94, 124 (1973) BEM Case.

Violence

1. Juvenile Delinquency Hearings, U.S. Senate Committee on the Judiciary, June, 1961, pg. 1637

2. Ibid. pg. 1637

3. Juvenile Delinquency Hearings, U.S. Senate Committee on the Judiciary, January 24, 1962, pg. 2406

4. Ibid.

5. Opening statement Senator Pastore, Mar. 21, 1972, Hearings Subcommittee on Commerce, second session; *Surgeon General's Report by Scientific Committee on Television and Social Behavior.*

6. Ibid.

7. Ibid.

8. Ibid.

9. Harry Castleman and Walter J. Podrazik, *Schedule Book: Four Decades of Network Programs from Sign-on- to Sign-off* (New York: McGraw-Hill, 1984).

10. *Brandenberg v. Ohio* 395 U.S. 444 (1969).

11. *New York University Magazine,* 1992, p. 34.

Sex

1. Philip Slater, *Pursuit of Loneliness* (New York: Beacon Press, 1970, 1976, p. 67.).

2. Ibid. p. 100

3. *Juvenile Delinquency Hearings, U.S. Senate Committee on the Judiciary,* Jan. 24, 1962, p. 243.

Editing Theatrical Movies for Television

1. "Family Viewing in Prime Time," ABC Television Network policy statement, Jan. 8, 1975.

Programs Designed for Children

1. Jules Power, *How Life Begins* (New York: Simon & Schuster, 1965).
2. The series was produced by Newall and Yohe Productions for Scholastic Rock, a subsidiary of McCaffrey and McCall.
3. Para. 28 & 31, 50 FCC second 829, 842 (1975).
4. *National Association of Independent Television Producers and Distributors v. FCC*, 516 F2 #526, 540.

Special Interest Advocacy

1. Kathryne Montgomery, *Target Prime Time, Advocacy Groups and the Struggle over Entertainment Television* (New York: Oxford Univ. Press, 1989), 13–14.
2. Christopher H. Sterling and John M. Kittross, *Stay Tuned: A Concise History of American Broadcasting*, (Belmont, Calif.: Wadworth Publishing, 1978).
3. "Minow Supports Amnesty to Hiss," *New York Times*, Nov. 19, 1962.

"The Family Viewing Hour"

1. Television Code 2.3 (18 ed. June 1975).
2. Geoffrey Cowan, *See No Evil*, (New York: Simon & Schuster, 1979), 147–48.
3. Memorandum opinion: Judge Warren S. Ferguson. *Writers Guild of America v. FCC and Tandem Productions Inc v. CBS et al.* USDC Central District California.
4. *Broadcasting/Cable*, Nov. 15, 1999, p. 24.

A Television Ratings System

1. *U.S. News & World Report*, story page; CNN interactive, CNN.com, July 10, 1997.
2. Ibid.
3. Ibid.

Speaking the Truth

1. The substance of this chapter appeared as an essay in the one hundredth issue of *The Television Quarterly, Journal of the National Academy of Television Arts and Sciences*, vol. 26, November 2, 1992
2. Daniel Aaron, "What Can Yo Learn from a Historical Novel?" American Heritage, Oct. 1992:55
3. Co-sponsored by the Nation Institute and the Center for American Culture Studies at Columbia Univ. in association with The Writers Guild East, as reported in *New York Times*, Mar. 3, 1992.
4. Bob Woodward and Carl Bernstein, *The Final Days* (New York: Simon & Schuster, 1976) 422–424.
5. Henry Kissinger, *Years of Upheaval* (Boston: Little, Brown, 1982) 1207–10.
6. *Red Lion Broadcasting Co. vs. FCC*, 395 U.S. 367 (1969).
7. David S. Versfelt, "The Fairness Doctrine: The End is Near," *Advertising Compliance*

Service, Greenwood Press, a division of Congressional Information Services, vol. 6 no. 22, Nov. 17, 1986, p. 5.

Censorship and the Censor's Role

1. Section 326 (47 U.S.C. 326) Communications Act of 1934.

2. Section 307 (47 U.S.C. 307) Communications Act of 1934.

3. *Red Lion Broadcasting Co. v. FCC,* 395 U.S. 367 (1969).

4. Sterling and Kittross, 126–32, 187–92.

5. T. Barton Carter, Marc A. Franklin, and Jay Be Wright, "The First Amendment and the Fourth Estate," in *The Law of Mass Media,* 7th ed (New York: Foundation Press, 1997), 798.

6. *FCC v. Pacifica Foundation,* 438 U.S. 726 (1978).

Index

A (Schneider's proposed label), 118
Aaron, Daniel, 122
ABC (American Broadcasting
    Companies): action-adventure
    programs, 13, 18; broadcast of
    theatrical movies, 46; code of standards
    and practices, 33; concern for
    children's programming, 75–76, 77;
    criteria for docudramas, 125–26; desire
    for objective program content review,
    21; direct control over entertainment
    programming, 2; and Family Viewing
    Hour, 103–4, 107, 109, 112, 113;
    finances, 17; importance of power of
    prime-time ratings, 37; importance of
    younger viewers to, 28; lack of
    affiliates, 20, 135; merger with United
    Paramount Theaters, xiii; method of
    coding violence, 21–22; network
    latecomer, ix, 135; on-air advisories,
    117–18; policy on special-interest
    groups and advertiser defections, 92;
    policy on violence and sex, 104–6;
    research on effects of violence, 15,
    18–19, 20–21; response to Pastore
    hearings, 16; Social Research unit, 4, 64;
    statement about *Soap*, 39–40. *See also*
    Broadcast Standards and Practices
    Department; Heller, Melvin; Polsky,
    Samuel; Schneider, Alfred
ABC Afterschool Specials, The (television
    shows), 7, 82
ABC Evening Report (news program), 91
ABC Weekend Specials (children's television
    shows), 80
ABC Workshop for Children's Television,
    76–77

abortion show (episode of *Maude*), xii
Academy of Television Arts and Sciences,
    96
action-adventure cartoons, 6–7. *See also*
    cartoons
action-adventure programming, 13
Action for Children's Television (ACT), 6
action programs, 3, 100
adult subject matter. *See* sexuality
    (depiction on television)
Adventures in Paradise (anthology series),
    12
advertisers, 49, 80–81, 90–93, 96
advisories, on-air: ABC's policy statement
    on, 104; ABC's use of, 117–18; for *The
    Day After*, 66; for "My Mom's Having a
    Baby," 82; required by Family Viewing
    Hour policy, 109; Schneider's views on,
    49; for *Soap*, 40; for *Something About
    Amelia*, 58. *See also* disclosures, on-air
affiliate stations, 20, 30, 31–32, 100
age appropriateness, 77
aggressive fantasies, 20–21
Ahls, Deborah, 40, 41
Alger, Ian, 64
Allen, Irwin, 85
Allen, Woody, 5, 48–50
All in the Family (television show): effects
    of Family Viewing Hour on, 112;
    Hobson's views on, 103–4; as icon
    of sex, 103, 108; issues in, 35, 100;
    realism, x
"All Star Saturday Kids," 80
American Broadcasting Companies. *See*
    ABC
American Business Consultants, 90
American Family Association, 96

American Gas Association, 91
American Horse, George, 69
American Legal Foundation, 63
American Psychiatric Association, 95
Americans, dichotomy about sexuality, 4
Americans for Responsible Television, 97
"America Rock," 80
Amiotte, George, 69
Anastasia, Albert, 94
animated cartoons. *See* cartoons
Annenberg, Walter, 91
Annie Hall (movie), 5, 48–50
Antczak, Al, 39
anthologies series, 12
antidrug messages, 98
antisocial modeling, 78
appointment viewing, 49
Archanbault, Joalln, 68
Archerd, Army, 52
Arledge, Roone, 63
Arnold, Danny, 8, 95, 111–12, 113, 138
Attica (docudrama), 127
audience participation shows, 74
authors, 72, 123
Avengers,The (television show), 18
Aware Inc., 90

Bad Wound, Louis, 68
balanced breakfast requirement, 81–82
Bank Street College of Education, 77, 78,
    79–80
Baretta (television show), 25, 117–18
Barney Miller (television show), 95, 111, 138
Barron, Arthur, 52
Beechold, Henry P., 80
beneficial violence, 17. *See also* gratuitous
    violence
Bernstein, Bob, 126
"Bigfoot and Wildboy," 80
births, shown on TV, xi, 82
blacklisting, 90
blacks, depiction in children's
    programming, 80
Blake, Robert, 25, 117
"Blind Sunday" (episode of *The ABC
    Afterschool Specials*), 82
blue penciling, 138

Bocho, Stephen, 139
Bogdanovich, Peter, 5, 31
Born Innocent (made-for-television movie),
    24, 101
Brauner, Julie, xiii
Breaking Point (television show), 13
breast feeding, 43
Briggs, Harry, Jr. (fict.), 127
Briggs, Mrs. (fict.), 127
broadcasting, 132
Broadcasting & Cable (magazine), 117, 119
broadcasting industry. *See* television
    industry
broadcast licenses, 9, 10, 132, 134
Broadcast Standards and Practices
    Department (BS&P, ABC): advisory for
    Annie Hall, 49; changing role of, 57;
    concerns about *War and Remembrance*,
    70, 71; difficulty of role, 137–38;
    function, 137; importance of guidelines
    to, 20; increased responsibility, xiv;
    lines of reporting, 136; response to
    stereotypical gay characters, 95;
    responsibility for Sunday evening
    programming, 84, 85; role in
    development of *Attica*, 127; role in
    development of *Superfriends*, 78; role in
    development of *The Day After*, 58, 60,
    64; views on *The Execution of Raymond
    Graham*, 72
"Broadcast Standards Editing" (ABC), 101
Brode, Harold, 60–61
Brodkin, Herbert, xi
Brooks, Richard, 5, 51, 52
Brown vs. Board of Education, 127–28
Bruce, Lenny, 28
BS&P. *See* Broadcast Standards and
    Practices Department
Buckley, William F., Jr., 63
Burger, Warren, 10
Burke, Chris, 86
Bus Stop (television show), 12

cable television, 48, 51
Caldecott, Helen, 64
Capital Cities Inc., 136
capital punishment, 72–73

Captain Kangaroo (children's television show), 74

Carlin, George, 134

cartoons, 6, 77. *See also* action-adventure cartoons

cathartic violence. *See* beneficial violence

Caucus of Writers, Producers and Directors, 96

CBS (Columbia Broadcasting System): direct control over entertainment programming, 2; policy on depictions of violence, 101; programming of *60 Minutes*, 83; reasons for promoting Family Viewing Hour, 103; shift in programming direction, 19; social research department, 4

censors: achievement of balance, 9; authority in twenty-first century, xii; changing role of, 39, 140; context for actions, 133; as corporate conscience, 136; and docudramas, 9; as editors, 102, 131; expansion of acceptable television, 45; as gatekeepers, 39; need for, 140–41; possible disappearance, 131; power, ix; questions of role of, 5; relationships with producers, 109; relationship to ratings system, 119; roles, 1, 7, 131–41; television program review, 8. *See also* Schneider, Alfred

censorship: changing dynamics of, 5; complicated nature, 118; demise, 132; general issues, 1; negotiation and compromise in, 138; relationship to freedom of expression, 5; relationship to public interest, 134–35. *See also* television ratings systems

cereals, 81–82

Charlie's Angels (television show), 35

Charren, Peggy, 6, 76, 80

checks and balances, 141

Cheyenne (television show), 12

child abuse, 45

children, 64–65, 75, 86

children's programming, 74–86; advertising guidelines, 80–81; changes to Saturday morning cartoons, 79–80; content, 6; FCC's definition of, 84; guidelines for, 78–79, 88; importance, 6;

need for improvement in mid-1970s, 76; new sources of, 87; on Sunday evenings, 83–84

"Children's Programming" (Futterman), 79

Children's Television Act (1990), 87, 134

choice, 124

Christian Anti-Communism Crusade, 90

Christian Leaders for Responsible Television, 96

Chunksa-Yua, 67

city-street violence, 100

Clark, Dick, 2

Clifford, Clark, 91

Clinton, William Jefferson, 87

Close, Glen, 41

Cochran, Ron, 91

Code, The. *See* National Association of Broadcasters Television Code

Code Authority. *See* National Association of Broadcasters Code Authority

Code Board. *See* National Association of Broadcasters Television Code Review Board

Code Review Board. *See* National Association of Broadcasters Television Code Review Board

Coffin, Thomas, 14

Collector, The (movie), 18

Collins, LeRoy, 92

Collum, John, 65

comedic violence, 6

comedy, in children's programming, 79

Communications Act of 1927, 132

Communications Act of 1934, 129, 132

Communications Act of 1992, 132

communications business, 131

conflict, basis of storytelling, 79

Congress. *See* U.S. Congress

consensus, importance of, 9

Cop Rock (television show), 139

cop shows, 12

counterprogramming, 28

Court of Appeals for the Ninth Circuit, 113

Cowan, Geoffrey, 111

Cowan, Louis G., xiii, 74

crime, 11. *See also* violence

critics, 75

Crystal, Billy, 36, 38, 95–96, 138
culture wars, 7
Curtis, Dan, 42, 69, 70, 71

D (television rating), 116
damn, acceptability of word, 110–11
Damon, Cathryn, 38
Danson, Ted, 41
Dark Shadows (television show), 18
Davis, John W., 127
Day After, The (movie of the week):
    children's response to, 63–66, 86;
    controversy over, 58–67; development
    guidelines, 59–60; placement of
    advertising in, 63; questions of taste in,
    62; ratings, 66; scientific issues, 60–62;
    viewer response, 66
Defenders,The, (television show), xi
democracy, 140
diaper changing, 43
diaphragm, prohibition of term, 62
Dieter, Newt, 95
Diller, Barry, 5, 6, 31, 33, 56
disclosures, on-air, 128
Discovery (children's television show),
    75
docudramas: ABC's criteria for, 125–26;
    Attica, 127; battle over, 140; dangers of,
    9; *The Final Days*, 126–27; impact, 128;
    importance of accurate treatment of
    issues, 124; influence on news practices
    and guidelines, 2; *JFK*, 123–25;
    preserving integrity of, 122–30;
    question of point of view, 128; *Separate
    but Equal*, 127–28. *See also* Fairness
    Doctrine
documentaries, 2
Dodd, Thomas, 11, 12, 13, 33
Dodd hearings, 29
"Don't Drink and Drive" campaign, 97–98
Doogie Howser, M.D. (television show), 139
drama, relevancy to political fears, 59
dramatic license, 122–23
Duffy, James, 76
Dutch (Morris), 122
Dynomitt (children's television show),
    80

Earth Day, 98
economic boycotts, 93
editing theatrical movies. *See* theatrical
    movies, editing for television
editorial judgment, 120–21
editors, roles, 102. *See also* censors
Eisenhower, Milton, 14
Eisenhower Commission on Violence
    (National Commission on the Causes
    and Prevention of Violence), 14, 17
Eisner, Michael, 6–7, 77
EMP (electro magnetic pulse), 61
enriched foods, 81
entertainment, 45, 57, 124
entertainment editors, 9
entertainment programming, 2, 4, 93
Epstein, Edward Jay, 124–25
equal time for political candidates, 129
Erlick, Everett, 14, 19
essential truth, 140
excess, as guideline for censorship, 137
excessive violence on television, 26, 137.
    See also violence (depiction on
    television)
Execution of Raymond Graham, The (made-
    for-television movie), 72–73
expletives, 48. *See also* words, unacceptable
exposition, 72

F (Schneider's proposed label), 118
Fabian, 12
fact and fiction, 9, 122, 124–25. *See also*
    docudramas
Fairness Doctrine, 128–29, 134
Falwell, Jerry, 62–63
Family Viewing Hour, 100–114; ABC
    policy statement on, 104–6;
    administration of policies of, xiv; birth
    of, 25, 108–9; congressional pressure
    for reinstatement, 119; constitutional
    status, 8; context, 100–101; court's
    defeat of, 36; culmination of battle over
    violence, 4; effects on *All in the Family*,
    112; effects on *Barney Miller*, 111–12;
    federal district court decision on, 82;
    lack of specifics in policy for, 110;
    meetings to formulate, 107–8; policy

statement, 109; potential damage to
ABC, 103–4; Schneider's opposition to,
102; suit by producers against, 113;
Television Code Review Board's
debates about, 8, 102–3
Family Viewing Policy. *See* Family
Viewing Hour
fantasy, as defuser of violence, 18
father-daughter sexual relationships, 5,
40–41
Faulk, John Henry, 90
Fay (television show), 112
FCC. *See* Federal Communications
Commission
Federal Communications Commission
(FCC): adoption of Pacifica ruling, 97;
approval of ABC–United Paramount
Theaters merger, xiii; Fairness
Doctrine, 128–29; power over indecent
speech, 134–35; Prime Time Access
Rules, 83; report on Family Viewing
Policy, 113–14; requirements under
Telecommunications Act, 115–16;
response to Children's Television Act,
87; review of television station
ownership, 20; Second Report and
Order Docket #19622 (on Sunday
evening children's programming), 84,
85; target of complaints about
television, 100–101
Ferguson, Warren, 103, 107–8, 113
Ferrell, Conchata, 35
fiction, distinction from nonfiction, 9, 122,
124–25. *See also* docudramas
"Filthy Words" (Carlin), 134
"Final Days" (docudrama), 9
Final Days, The (docudrama), 126–27
First Amendment, 24, 132, 133
First Amendment freedoms, 12
Ford, Gerald R., Jr., 91
"Francesca Baby" (episode of *The ABC
Afterschool Specials*), 82
Frawley, Patrick J., 90, 91, 93
freedom of expression, 5, 104–5
freedom of speech, 24, 98, 133
Friendly Fire (movie of the week), 57
fundamentalist special-interest groups, 96
Futterman, Susan, 79, 85

Fuzz (television show), 22–23
FV (television rating), 116

G (television rating), 115
G (theatrical movie rating), 47
Gale, Max, 111
Garraty, John A., 80
Gay Activist Alliance, 94–95
gay and lesbian community, 7, 39, 94–95.
See also homosexuality
gay characters, 111. *See also Soap*
Gay Media Task Force, 95
Gelbart, Larry, 113
Gentleman's Agreement (Hobson), 35
Gerbner, George, 26
Gere, Richard, 51
Giago, Tim, 69
Gold, Ron, 94–95
Goldberg, Leonard, 5, 25, 40–42
Goldenson, Isabelle, 89
Goldenson, Leonard: awareness of
audience desires, 28; charge to
Schneider, 2; congressional testimony,
2; leadership of ABC, xiii–xiv; response
to *All in the Family*, 35; role in
controversy over *Profiles of Courage*,
91–92; sit-in in office of, 94–95
government, 2. *See also* U.S. Congress
Graduate, The (movie), 30, 32
Graham, Robin, 47, 52, 69
"Grammar Rock," 80
gratuitous violence, 17, 23, 105
Guardella, Kay, 36
guns, 137. *See also* violence (depiction on
television)
Gunsmoke (Western), 12

Hagerty, Jim, 90, 92
Haines, Randa, 41
Hanley, Bill, 41
Hanta Yo (Hill), 67
Hanta Yo (made-for-television movie),
67–68. *See also Mystic Warrior*
Hardy Boys (television series), 85
Harris, Mel, 43
Harris, Susan, 36, 37, 38, 112

Heffner, Richard, 51, 52, 53–54
hell, use of word, 110–11
Heller, Melvin: characterization of
  thirtysomething, 42; concern over
  content of *The Day After,* 64;
  consultation on Sunday evening
  children's programs, 85; defense of
  Toma episode, 30–31; development of
  criteria to evaluate television material,
  17–19; development of Incident
  Classification and Analysis Form, 22;
  research on television violence, 21;
  review of *The Last Picture Show,* 32;
  review of *Looking for Mr. Goodbar,* 52;
  review of programming, 106; role in
  changing Saturday morning
  programming, 77; role in script of *That
  Certain Summer,* 33–34; *Sexuality,
  Television and Broadcast Standards,*
  96–97; warning about increased
  emphasis on sex, 29
Hellfrich, Stockton, 17, 12, 109, 110
Helmond, Katherine, 38
Helms, Jesse, 138
Henry, Natalie (fict.), 70
Herskowitz, Marshall, 43, 44, 45
Hier, Marvin, 69–70
Hill, Ruth Beebe, 67, 68
Hill Street Blues (television show), 139
Hinson, Hal, 24–25
Hiss, Alger, 90–91
historical novels, 122
Hobson, Laura Z., 35, 103–4
Holbrook, Hal, 33
Holocaust. *See War and Remembrance*
homosexual affection, 43, 44
homosexuality, 6, 13, 33–34, 36. *See also* gay
  and lesbian community
homosexual relationships, 33
Hooks, William, 78
Hoover, Julie, 36, 52
Hot l Baltimore (television show), 35
House Un-American Activities
  Committee, 90–91
Howdy Doody (television show), 74
Howe, Mark Dewolf, 71
"How Life Begins" (Power), 75
Hudson, Rock, 43

Humanitas Committee, 98
Hume, Ed, 60
humor, mitigator of violence, 3, 18, 79

idea placement, 98
"If We Must Rate TV, Let's Get It Right"
  (Schneider), 117
immorality, 37
incest, 40, 41–42, 138. *See also* sexuality
Incident Classification and Analysis Form
  (ICAF), 22
Independent Television Association, 108
infant nudity, 43
information, distinction from propaganda,
  93
Internet, 86, 131
Invaders, The (television show), 18
invention, place in docudramas, 125
Irvine, Reed, 62–63
Italian-Americans, 94
I Will Fight No More Forever (made-for-
  television movie), 67

Jaffee, Charles, 48–49
Jaffee, Louis Leventhal, xiii
Jastrow, Aaron (fict), 70, 71
Jeffersons, The (television show), x, 100
JFK (movie), 123–24
jiggle TV, 35
Joseph, Chief, 67
journalistic integrity, 90–93

Kaiser, Ellwood, 98
Kearl, Wayne, 102
Keaton, Diane, 51
Keeshan, Bob, 74
Keever, Jake, 63
Kemper Insurance Companies, 91
Kennedy, John F., 91, 123–24
Kersey, Tom, 58, 78–79
Kinte, Kunte (fict.), 138
Kintner, Robert, xiii
Kissinger, Henry, 63, 126–27
Klapper, Joseph, 12, 14
Klute (movie), 30, 32

KONO-TV, 29
Koppel, Ted, 63
Kraft Theater, The , x

L (Schneider's proposed label), 118
L (television rating), 116
labeling system, 118–19
Landsberg, Allan, 45
language. *See* words, unacceptable
Last Picture Show, The (movie), 5, 30,
    31–33
Leachman, Cloris, 31
Lear, Norman, 8, 35, 112, 113
lesbians, violence against, 23
Levinson (producer of *Columbo*), 33
Lewis, Dorothy Otnow, 26
Lewis, Jerry, 89
Lieberman Research Inc., 18
Life (magazine), 57
Life Goes On (television show), 86
lift scenes, 47
Link, Bill, 33
"Lion Walks among Us, A" (*Bus Stop*
    episode), 12, 28–29
Little Ladies of the Night (movie of the
    week), 57
Lometti, Guy, 22
Long Day's Journey into Night (O'Neill), 30
Look (magazine), 57
Looking for Mr. Goodbar (movie), 5, 51–53
Lowe, Chad, 86
loyalty oaths, 90
Lucky Strike cigarettes, 94
Lyons, Oren, 68

MA (Schneider's proposed label), 118
made-for-television movies. *See* movies
    made for television
Mafia, ABC's use of word, 94
Marcus Welby, M.D. (television show), 7,
    30, 95
Marguiles, Stan, 67
Married with Children (television show),
    97
Marshall, Thurgood, 127
Martin, Kellie, 86

M*A*S*H (television show), 100
mature subject matter, 118
Maude (television show), x, xii, 35,
    100
Maytag, Ann, 68
McCall, David, 79–80
McCarthy, Joseph, 91
McKenna, Jim, 19
McNamara, Robert S., 63
Means, Russell, 68
media, 6, 97
Mexican-Americans, 80
Meyer, Nicholas, 62
Michaels, Bob, 42
Midnight Cowboy (movie), 30, 32, 50
Miller, John, 74
miniseries, 72
minorities, 78, 80
Minow, Newton, 92
Mobile Two (movie), 110–11
Mod Squad, The (television show), 3
Moonlighting (television show), 35
Moore, Thomas, 13
Morality in Media (special interest group),
    7
Moral Majority, 96
Morris, Edmund, 122
Motion Picture Association of America,
    117
Motion Picture Association of America,
    Classification and Rating
    Administration, 46, 51
Motion Picture Code (Motion Picture
    Association of America), 46
motion pictures. *See* movies
movie producers, 28
movies, 5–6. *See also* movies made for
    television; theatrical movies
movies made for television, 56–73; *The Day
    After*, 58–67; *The Execution of Raymond
    Graham*, 72–73; importance, 73;
    influences on acceptable content or
    language, 4; *Mystic Warrior*, 67–69; *War
    and Remembrance*, 42, 69–72
movies of the week (MOWs), 5, 56–57. *See
    also The Day After*
Moviolas (editing machines), 31
MOWs. *See* movies of the week

Mr. Rodgers' Neighborhood (children's
    television show), 74–75
Mulligan, Richard, 38
"Multiplication Rock," 79–80
Murrow, Edward R., 91
"My Mom's Having a Baby" (episode of
    The ABC Afterschool Specials), 82
Mystic Warrior (made-for-television
    movie), 67–69

NAB (National Association of
    Broadcasters), x, 109
NAB Code. *See* National Association of
    Broadcasters Television Code
Nabrit, James, 127
NAITPD case, 84
Naked City (television show), 12
Nancy Drew (television show), 85
National Association of Broadcasters
    (NAB), x, 109
National Association of Broadcasters Code
    Authority: approval for *The Last Picture
    Show*, 32; authority and responsibility,
    xiv; end of, 82, 114; monitoring system,
    13, 110; oversight of entertainment
    programming, xiv
National Association of Broadcasters Code
    Authority Director, 106, 110
National Association of Broadcasters
    Television Code, 13, 30, 33, 114
National Association of Broadcasters
    Television Code Review Board:
    consideration of Family Viewing Hour,
    102–3; demise, 82; guidelines for
    children's advertising, 80–81; role in
    implementation of Family Viewing
    Hour, 110; Schneider's service on, x,
    xiv, 8; standards on violence, 13. *See
    also* National Association of
    Broadcasters Television Code
National Commission on the Causes and
    Prevention of Violence (Eisenhower
    Commission), 14, 17
National Education Association, 64
National Gay Task Force, 94
Native Americans, 67
NBC (National Broadcasting Company):

direct control over entertainment
    programming, 2; guidelines on
    depictions of violence, 101;
    participation in television ratings
    system, 116; pioneer of movies made
    for television, 56; social research
    department, 4; suit against, 24; Sunday
    evening children's programs, 83, 85;
    support for Family Viewing Hour idea,
    106–7; vulnerability to criticism over
    violence in *Born Innocent*, 101
NC-17 (theatrical movie rating), 47
Neaman, Milton, xiii
Nelson, Ozzie, 29
network executives, 11–12
networks: commitment to Family Viewing
    Hour, 113; defense of television, 22;
    dominance, 45, 114; expansion of
    departments of standards and
    practices, 2; response to government
    pressure over depictions of violence,
    102–3; voluntary nature, 132. *See also*
    ABC; CBS; NBC
news, blurring of entertainment with,
    57
news editors, 8–9
news programs, 2, 92
New Yorker cartoon, 27
New York Times, 29
Nez Percé, 67
Nichols, Mike, 32
1950s, 2
1970s, x, 20, 27–28, 30, 76, 100–101
ninety-minute movies, 6
Nixon, Richard, 9, 101, 126, 127
novels for television, 80
no violence and no sex zone. *See* Family
    Viewing Hour
noxious violence. *See* gratuitous violence
nuclear war. *See The Day After*
nudity, as death, 71
"Nuremberg Trials, The," 91
Nurses, The (television show), xi

O'Connor, Carroll, 35
Oglala Sioux, 67
Ojai, California, 123

Olin, Ken, 43
on-air advisories. *See* advisories, on-air
Onassis, Jacqueline Kennedy, 9
One Step Beyond (anthology series), 12
oral sex, 71
original theatrical motion pictures. *See*
    theatrical movies
Oswald, Russell, 127
Otto, Linda, 45
Outlaws, The (television show), 12
Ozzie and Harriet (television show), 29
"Ozzie's Girls," 29

Pacifica Foundation, 134
Pacifica ruling (seven dirty words), 97,
    134–35
Paley, William S., xiii, 91
Papazian, Robert, 62
parental supervision, 131. *See also* parents
parents, 26, 82–83, 117, 121
Parker, Everett, 36
participation buys (advertising method),
    94
Pastore, John O., 3, 14, 15
Patton (theatrical movie), 138–39
payola scandals, xiii–xiv, 2
Pearson, Drew, 91
pedophilia, 95
People Next Door, The (television show),
    xi
PG-13 (theatrical movie rating), 47
PG (theatrical movie rating), 47
pleasure, 27
Pleshette, Suzanne, 40
"Political Obituary of Richard M. Nixon,
    The" (news program), 90
Polsky, Samuel, 17–19, 21, 32, 33–34, 106
Postman, Neil, 86
Power, Jules, 75
"Power of the Historical Novel" (Aaron),
    122
pregnant, as word, x
preteens, 86
prime time, 19, 84
Prime Time Access Rules, 83, 85
prior restraint, 39
privacy, right to, 135

producers: response to Family Viewing
    Hour, 109–10; suit over Family
    Viewing Hour, 113
Profiles in Courage (Kennedy), 91
program departments, ix, x
programming decisions, 132–33
programs for children. *See* children's
    programming
Program Standards Committee (of
    National Association of Broadcasters
    Television Code Review Board), 107,
    110
pro-social programming, 6, 76, 87
PTA, 76
public, response to quiz show scandals, 2
public affairs programs, 134
public interest, 130, 132, 133–34, 135–36
public service propaganda, 97–98

Question of Love, A (movie of the week), 57
quiz show scandals, xiv, 2

R (theatrical movie rating), 47, 50, 117
rating systems, 26, 46, 47, 119. *See also*
    television ratings systems
*Red Channels: The Report of Communist
    Influence in Radio and Television*
    (American Business Consultants), 90
Red Lion case, 129, 133
Red Shirt, Larry, 68
Reiner, Rob, 35
Rekolta, Terry, 97
religious community, 39, 96
*Report on Editorializing by Broadcast
    Licensees* (FCC), 129
Review Board (for television ratings), 116
Reynolds, Burt, 22
Rich (representative of Duluth NBC
    affiliate), 107, 108
Rintels, David, 72, 123, 125
Robards, Jason, 61
role modeling, 77–78, 78
"Rookie of the Year" (episode of *The ABC
    Afterschool Specials*), 82
Rookies, The (television show), 3, 102, 103,
    108, 112

Roots (television miniseries), 3, 138
Rose, Reginald, xi
Roush, Matt, 139
Route 66 (television show), 12
R-rated movies, 5, 47, 50–51, 54
Rubenstein, Eli, 14, 19
Rubin, Ellis, 24
Rudd, Bobo, 71
Rule, Elton, 35
Rushnell, Squire, 80

S (Schneider's proposed label), 118
S (television rating), 116
safe harbor idea. *See* Family Viewing Hour
Sagan, Carl, 63
Salant, Dick, 92
Samuels, Stu, 58, 60
Sanford and Son (television show), x
Sarrel, Lorna, 97
Sarrel, Philip, 97
satire, 39
Saturday Evening Post, The (magazine), 57
Saturday morning cartoons, 6, 76, 79–80
Sauter, Van Gordon, 36–37
scarcity doctrine, 129, 133
Schneider, Alfred R.: advocacy for *Soap*, 39;
censoring of Jerry Lewis, 89; changing
role of, 57; clashes with homosexual
community, 7; decision to broadcast
Annie Hall, 49, 50; early career, xiii–xiv;
at Harvard Law School, xiii; influences
on, xi; limitations on action-adventure
programs, 21; mission to Frawley, 90,
92; objectives as censor, 4–5, 10;
opposition to safe harbor idea, 102;
participation in meeting about *Soap*, 36;
personal credo, 135–36; proposal for
labeling system, 118–19; relationship
with Spelling, 102; respect for, ix;
response to *All in the Family*, 35, 104;
response to proposal for Family
Viewing Hour, 103; response to
Something About Amelia, 41; review of
War and Remembrance, 42; service on
Television Code Review Board, 8; and
special-interest advocates, 7; support
for diverse program schedule, 21

—disputes, 44, 52–54, 72, 108, 111–12
—roles: at ABC, 1; as censor, 4–5; in
devising rating system, 117; in editing
of *Looking for Mr. Goodbar*, 52; in editing
theatrical movies, 47; in editing *The
Last Picture Show*, 31; on Program
Standards Committee, 107; in script of
That Certain Summer, 33–34
—views: on broadcasters' responsibilities,
82; on *The Day After*, 58, 63; on
disclosures, 128; on docudramas, 122;
on Fairness Doctrine, 128–30; on
Family Viewing Hour, 103, 108; on full
frontal nudity, 42; on gatekeeper
function, 25; on media accuracy, 97; on
movies made for television, 73; on
outside authority over programming,
107; on programs dealing with
interpersonal relationships, 30; on
public interest, 93–94; on role as censor,
136–37; on *Soap*, 36; on television
ratings systems, 115, 116–17, 119–21; on
television's proper role, 98; on
theatrical movie rating system, 53–54;
on truth in docudramas, 122–23; on
violence, 25
Schwarz, Fred, 90
Scientific Advisory Committee on
Television and Social Behavior, 14,
15–16
See No Evil (Cowan), 111
selective viewing, 49
self-regulation, 104, 120
Senate Committee on Commerce,
Subcommittee on Communications, 14
"Senator Targets Broadcast Licenses," 119
Separate but Equal (docudrama), 9,
127–28
sex education, 75
sex roles, 77–78
Sex Symbol, The (movie), 32
sexual comedies, 36–37
sexuality (depiction on television), 27–45;
censoring of, 137; in *Charlie's Angels*, 35;
complaints about, 4; controversy
about, 27; current explicitness, 45;
homosexuality in *That Certain Summer*,
33–34; in *The Last Picture Show*

(Bogdanovich), 31–33; in *Soap*, 36–40; in *Something About Amelia*, 40–41; source of conflict in late 1960s and early 1970s, 27–28; in *thirtysomething*, 42–45

Sexuality, Television and Broadcast Standards (Heller), 96–97

sexual references, 48

Seymour, Jane, 71

Shales, Tom, 50

Shephard, Cybil, 31, 35

Shultz, George, 63

Silverman, Fred, 36, 37

Singer, Dorothy, 63–64, 80

Singer, Jerome, 80

Six Million Dollar Man, The (television show), 4, 85, 112

60 Minutes (news program), 83

Slater, Philip, 27, 28

Sleeper (movie), 48

slow motion, 4

Smith, Howard K., 90–91

Smith, Sally Bedell, 91

Smothers, Tommy, x–xi

Smothers Brothers, The (television show), x

Soap (television show), 37–40; debate over, 38; depictions of homosexuals on, 95–96; depictions of sexuality on, 36–37; intended audience, 37; religious right's response to, 96; as satire, x

social and political changes, late 1960s and early 1970s, 20

social issues, 100

social problems, xi

social reality shows, xi

social research departments, 4, 17

Something About Amelia (television drama), 5, 40–41, 58

Sorenson, Ted, 91

Soviet Union, 67

special interest advocacy, 89–99, 90, 93

special-interest advocates, 7, 38, 39

Spelling, Aaron, 25, 35, 102

sports programs, 2

standards, television's need to test, 32

standards and practices, 32. *See also* Broadcast Standards and Practices Department (BS&P, ABC); rating systems; television ratings systems

standards and practices departments, xii, 2, 119. *See also* Broadcast Standards and Practices Department (BS&P, ABC)

Stanton, Frank, xiv

Starksy and Hutch (television show), 25

Steinfeld, Jesse L., 16

Stephens, Kathy, 60

stereotypes, 78

Stern, Howard, 97

Stevens, George, Jr., 9

Stevens, John Paul, 134–35

Stith, Deborah Prothrow, 26

Stoddard, Brandon: and *The Day After*, 58, 62; discussions over violence in *Roots*, 3; influence on *War and Remembrance*, 42, 71; and *Something About Amelia*, 5, 40

Stone, Oliver, 123

Struthers, Sally, 35

Summer of '42 (movie), 32

Sunday evening programming, 76, 84–85

Superfriends (children's television show), 6–7, 77

Supreme Court, 129, 134–35

surgeon general, 14

Suskind, David, 36

Swafford, Tom, 103, 107, 108, 112

S.W.A.T (television show), 25

Szekely, Andre de, 5, 31, 47, 52

talk shows, xii

Taxi Driver (movie), 118

Taylor, Arthur, 101–2, 103

technological changes, 87

teenagers, 6. *See also* young teenagers

Telecommunications Act, 115–16

teleplays. *See* docudramas

television: as cause of crime and violence, 11, 24; conservatism, xi; importance in children's lives, 82; lightning rod for social controversies, 3; as mirror, 9; permissiveness, 29; proper role, 98; questions of social influence, 3; role in shaping majority standards, 37; in 1960s and 1970s, x, 20; as scapegoat, 101

television advertising, xii
Television and Families (quarterly
    newsletter), 34
television audience, 50
Television Code Review Board. *See*
    National Association of Broadcasters
    Television Code Review Board
television dramas, xi
television industry, 20
television morality, 29
television news, 2, 92
television programming, 28, 34
television ratings systems, 115–21;
    importance of editorial judgment, 120;
    limitations, 119–21; need for context,
    117; origins, 55; supporters, 116. *See also*
    rating systems
television sets, 11
television station licenses, 9, 10, 132, 134
television viewers, 7
television violence. *See* violence (depiction
    on television)
That Certain Summer (television drama), 6,
    33–34, 57
theatrical movies: ACB's policy statement
    on, 106; expense of licensing, 56;
    influences on television, 4; new source
    of program supply, 28; provocative, 30;
    rerating of R-rated, 50–51
theatrical movies, editing for television,
    46–55; *Annie Hall*, 48–50; *Looking for Mr.
    Goodbar*, 51–54; number of rerated R
    movies, 53; problems of, 5, 46–47
thirtysomething (television show), 42–45
three-hour rule, 19
Three's Company (television show), 35–36,
    137
Till Death Do Us Part (British television
    series), 35
Time (magazine), 38–39
Time to Die, A (Wicker), 127
tits and ass programming, 35
Toma (television show), 30
Traviesas, Herminio, 36, 107, 112
Treyz, Oliver, 12–13, 28, 89, 92
truth, 122, 140
TV. *See entries beginning "television"*
TV-14 (television rating), 115

TV-M (television rating), 115
TV-MA (television rating), 115
TV-PG (television rating), 115
TV-Y7 (television rating), 115
TV-Y (television rating), 115
Twilight Zone, The (television show), 12
Twin Peaks, 45

unacceptable words. *See* words,
    unacceptable
United States, pluralistic society, 98–99
unmarried couples, xi
Unmarried Woman, An (movie of the week),
    57
Unspeakable Acts (television show), 45
Untouchables, The (television show), 12,
    94
U.S. Congress, 3, 12, 101, 115. *See also* Dodd
    hearings; Pastore, John O.
U.S. Senate Subcommittee to Investigate
    Juvenile Delinquency, 11

V (television rating), 116
Valenti, Jack, 55
V-chips, 26, 115–16, 120
VCRs, 51
Viewpoint (ABC news program), 63
violence, 11, 13, 14, 23, 24, 114
violence (depiction on television), 11–26;
    ABC policy statement on, 104; ABC's
    guidelines on, 17–18; ABC's methods
    of coding, 21–22; continuing debate
    over, 8, 11, 101; effects, 26; in *Fuzz*,
    22–23; hearings on impact on children,
    13; importance of showing
    consequences, 18; need for guidelines
    on, 16; in 1960s and early 1970s, 100;
    Pastore hearings, 14–16; questions of
    effects on children, 75; questions of
    treatment of, 3; relationship to
    problems of violence, 120; response to
    congressional hearings on, 13;
    summary, 26. *See also* U.S. Senate
    Subcommittee to Investigate Juvenile
    Delinquency
violent relationships, 21

Wallace, Mike, 91
War and Remembrance (television
    miniseries), 42, 69–72, 138
war in Vietnam, 25
weekday afternoon programming, 76
Weiswasser, Stephen, 136, 140
Weitman, Bob, 89
West, Mae, 9
Westerns, 12
White, Bret, 44, 58, 60, 70–71
White, Steve, 58, 60
White, Ward, 70
Wicker, Tom, 127
Wiesel, Elie, 63
Wildmon, Donald, 7, 96
Wiley, Richard, 8, 101
Willis, Bruce, 35
Winchel, Walter, 91–92
Witt, Paul, 112
Wolper, David, 67, 68
Woman's Room, The (movie of the week), 57
women, open discussion of sexuality by,
    38
Wonder Woman, 7

Woodward, Carl, 126
words, unacceptable: *damn,* 110–11;
    diaphragm, 62; *hell,* 111; *nooky,* 139;
    Pacifica ruling, 97, 134–35; *pregnant,* x;
    scumbag, 139; use in *Patton,* 138–39
Wouk, Herman, 42
Writers Guild of America, 113
Wurtzel, Alan, 22

X rating (for theatrical movies), 47

Years of Upheaval (Kissinger), 126
Yeltsin, Boris, 67
young children, 75
young teenagers, 7, 82

Zall, Roxanna, 41
Zamora, Ronny, 24
Zapple, Nick, 15
Zorbaugh, Geraldine, xiii
Zwick, Ed, 43

The Television Series
Robert J. Thompson, Series Editor

Bonfire of the Humanities: Television, Subliteracy, and Long-Term Memory Loss. David Marc

Cue the Bunny on the Rainbow: Tales from TV's Most Prolific Sitcom Director. Alan Rafkin

"Deny All Knowledge": Reading the X Files. David Lavery, Angela Hague, and Marla Cartwright, eds.

Dictionary of Teleliteracy: Television's 500 Biggest Hits, Misses, and Events. David Bianculli

Framework: A History of Screenwriting in the American Film. Third Edition. Tom Stempel

Gen X TV: The Brady Bunch to Melrose Place. Rob Owen

King of the Half Hour: Nat Hiken and the Golden Age of Comedy. David Everitt

Laughs, Luck . . . and Lucy: How I Came to Create the Most Popular Sitcom of All Time. Jess Oppenheimer, with Gregg Oppenheimer

Living Room War. Michael J. Arlen

Lou Grant: The Making of TV's Top Newspaper Drama. Douglass K. Daniel

Prime-Time Authorship: Works about and by Three TV Dramatists. Douglas Heil

Prime Time, Prime Movers: From I Love Lucy to L.A. Law America's Greatest TV Shows and the People Who Created Them. David Marc and Robert J. Thompson

Rod Serling's Night Gallery: An After-Hours Tour. Scott Skelton and Jim Benson

The Story of Viewers for Quality Television: From Grassroots to Prime Time. Dorothy Collins Swanson

Storytellers to the Nation: A History of American Television Writing. Tom Stempel

Teleliteracy: Taking Television Seriously. David Bianculli

Television's Second Golden Age: From Hill Street Blues to ER. Robert J. Thompson

TV Creators: Conversations with America's Top Producers of Television Drama. James L. Longworth, Jr.

The View from Highway 1: Essays on Television. Michael J. Arlen